Lecture Notes in Computer Science 10727

Commenced Publication in 1973
Founding and Former Series Editors:
Gerhard Goos, Juris Hartmanis, and Jan van Leeuwen

More information about this series at http://www.springer.com/series/7409

Jaap Ham · Anna Spagnolli
Benjamin Blankertz · Luciano Gamberini
Giulio Jacucci (Eds.)

Symbiotic Interaction

6th International Workshop, Symbiotic 2017
Eindhoven, The Netherlands, December 18–19, 2017
Revised Selected Papers

 Springer

Editors
Jaap Ham (ID)
Department of Innovation Sciences
Eindhoven University of Technology
Eindhoven, Noord-Brabant
The Netherlands

Anna Spagnolli
University of Padua
Padua
Italy

Benjamin Blankertz
TU Berlin
Berlin, Berlin
Germany

Luciano Gamberini
University of Padua
Padua
Italy

Giulio Jacucci
Department of Computer Science
University of Helsinki
Helsinki
Finland

ISSN 0302-9743   ISSN 1611-3349 (electronic)
Lecture Notes in Computer Science
ISBN 978-3-319-91592-0   ISBN 978-3-319-91593-7 (eBook)
https://doi.org/10.1007/978-3-319-91593-7

Library of Congress Control Number: 2018942347

LNCS Sublibrary: SL3 – Information Systems and Applications, incl. Internet/Web, and HCI

Printed on acid-free paper

This Springer imprint is published by the registered company Springer International Publishing AG part of Springer Nature
The registered company address is: Gewerbestrasse 11, 6330 Cham, Switzerland

Preface

Symbiotic interaction can be achieved by combining computation, sensing technology, and interaction design to realize deep perception, awareness, and understanding between humans and computers. In this highly multidisciplinary research domain, distributed systems are studied that can easily and autonomously sense the physiological and behavioral information of users over time, and can use this information in its relationship with users, while the user interacts with the system, understanding it regardless of his/her ability to explicitly refine his/her request.

The International Workshop on Symbiotic Interaction is the primary venue for presenting scientific work dealing with the symbiotic relationships between humans and computers and for discussing the nature and implications of such relationships. At this small yet gritty workshop, researchers from academia and industry from all over the world discuss the latest theories, research findings, issues, applications, and artifacts related to this kind of interaction, acknowledged as qualitatively different from other kinds of human interdependency with technologies considered in the past. Previous editions of the workshop were held in Padua (twice), London, Helsinki, and Berlin. A description of the workshop series and its focus can be found at www.symbiotic-interaction.org.

SYMBIOTIC 2017 was organized by Eindhoven University of Technology and was held in Eindhoven (The Netherlands) during December 18–19. At least two reviewers from a scientific committee of 24 experts in the different areas covered by this workshop evaluated each submission. Of the 23 submitted papers, ten were accepted, yielding an acceptance rate of 43.8%. Among these, the work presented by Giulia Cartocci et al., "Alpha and Theta EEG Variations as Indices of Listening Effort to Be Implemented in Neurofeedback Among Cochlear Implant Users," won the Best Paper award. The program included three keynotes by Elisabeth André, Anne-Marie Brouwer, and Pim Haselager.

This volume contains the accepted short and long papers presented during the main track of the conference. In addition, the volume includes the abstracts of the keynote speeches and a report of the special panel on ethics that has become a tradition in this workshop and that this year was devoted to discussing "Transparency as an Ethical Safeguard."

This conference was only a success thanks to the great efforts of many people. We thank our sponsors for their involvement and participation in the meeting: BrainProducts, Center for Humans and Technology (TU/e), TMSi, and Noldus Information Technology. We would like to thank all authors for submitting their high-quality work, the reviewers for their constructive and extensive feedback, and all scientific and organizational chairs who worked hard to allow this conference to be such an important addition to scientific knowledge and the research and practice communities studying symbiotic interaction.

December 2017

Jaap Ham
Anna Spagnolli
Benjamin Blankertz
Luciano Gamberini
Giulio Jacucci

Organization

General Chairs

Jaap Ham   Eindhoven University of Technology, The Netherlands
Anna Spagnolli   University of Padua, Italy

Program Chairs

Benjamin Blankertz   Technische Universität Berlin, Germany
Luciano Gamberini   University of Padua, Italy
Giulio Jacucci   University of Helsinki, Finland

Associate Chair

Jonathan Freeman   Goldsmiths College University of London, UK

DC Chair

Elisabeth André   Augsburg University, Germany

Sponsorship Chair

Benjamin Blankertz   Technische Universität Berlin, Germany

Website Chair

Sitwat Langrial   Sur University College, Oman

Communications Assistant

Diletta Mora   University of Padua, Italy

Liaison Chairs

Fabio Babiloni   University of Rome Sapienza and BrainSigns Srl, Italy
Joel Fischer   Nottingham University, UK
Anthony Jameson   DFKI, German Research Center for Artificial
                              Intelligence/International University in Germany
Bilge Mutlu   University of Wisconsin-Madison, USA
Erin Treacy Solovey   Drexel University, USA

Program Committee

Elisabeth André	Augsburg University, Germany
Ilkka Arminen	University of Helsinki, Finland
Jose Barata	Universidade Nova de Lisboa, Portugal
Anne-Marie Brouwer	TNO Human Factors – Perceptual and Cognitive Systems
Marc Cavazza	University of Kent, UK
Ricardo Chavarriaga	Ecole Polytechnique Federale de Lausanne, Switzerland
Marco Congedo	GIPSA-lab, CNRS and Grenoble University, France
Mauro Conti	University of Padua, Italy
Peter Desain	Radboud University Nijmegen and Donders Institute for Brain, Cognition and Behaviour, The Netherlands
Stephen Fairclough	LJMU, UK
Jonathan Freeman	Goldsmiths College, University of London, UK
Dorota Glowacka	University of Helsinki, Finland
David Kirsh	University of California, San Diego, USA
Sitwat Langrial	Sur University College, Oman
Christian Licoppe	Telecom-ParisTech, France
Fabien Lotte	Inria Bordeaux Sud-Ouest/LaBRI, France
Juan C. Moreno	Consejo Superior de Investigaciones Científicas (CSIC), Spain
Aimee Robbins-Van Wynsberghe	University of Delft, The Netherlands
Reinhold Scherer	Graz University of Technology, Austria
Markus Wenzel	Technische Universität Berlin, Germany
Thorsten Zander	Technische Universität Berlin, Germany
Ivan Volosyak	Rhine-Waal University of Applied Sciences, Germany
Francesco Di Nocera	Sapienza University of Rome, Italy
Emanuele Menegatti	University of Padova, Italy
Yuan Zhang	University of Jinan, China

Additional Reviewers

Lena M. Andreessen	Technische Universität Berlin, Germany
Valeria Orso	University of Padova, Italy
Patrik Pluchino	University of Padova, Italy
Zahra Pooranian	University of Padova, Italy

Sponsors

Gold Sponsors

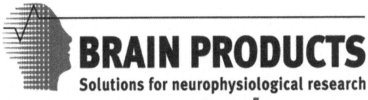

Silver Sponsors

Keynote Speakers Abstracts

Keynote Speakers Abstracts

Mental State Monitoring Using Physiological Signals to Evaluate Food Experience, Reduce Delays in Head-Mounted Displays, and Everything in Between

Anne-Marie Brouwer

The Netherlands Organization for Applied Scientific Research (TNO),
The Netherlands

In this talk I will present some of our recent work on exploiting (neuro) physiological signals as a source of information about individuals' cognitive and affective state. Potentially, such a continuous stream of information that can be obtained without distracting the individual, and without having to rely on verbal reports, is valuable in a wide range of applications. However, researchers in the field face some recurring challenges: (1) no simple mapping between physiology and mental state – issues of generalization (2) effects of body movement on physiology (3) estimates of mental state are imperfect – (how) can their benefit outweigh the costs? I will discuss our research along the lines of these challenges and how we tried to deal with them.

On the Ethics of Symbiotic Interaction Design: No Need to Say 'Ni'

Pim Haselager

Donders Institute for Brain, Cognition and Behaviour, Radboud University
Nijmegen, The Netherlands

Constructive ethics aims to investigate the ethical, legal and societal implications of emerging technologies in such a way that the major concerns of the major stakeholders are addressed early on in the research and design process. To illustrate this, I will focus on the implications of symbiotic technology for a user's sense of agency and responsibility for mediated action. The distinction between something I do and something that happens to me is generally clear, but not always an easy one to make. Increasingly we are embedded in environments full of artificial 'helpers' that actively contribute to the translation of human (sub)conscious intentions into action. While displaying a behavior, a user of symbiotic technology may be uncertain about being the agent of a genuine act. Symbiotic and neuroadaptive technologies have the potential to create new and fascinating cases where the question 'who did that?' will make sense individually and societally, with consequences for the assessment of ethical and legal responsibility.

Socially Sensitive Technologies for Symbiotic Human-Robot Interaction

Elizabeth André

Ausburg University, Germany

Societal challenges, such as an ageing population, have created the need for a new generation of robots that are able to smoothly interact with people in their daily environment. Such robots require a great amount of social intelligence including the capability to be attentive to the user's emotional state and respond to it appropriately. In the past ten years, an increasing amount of effort has been dedicated to explore the potential of affective computing in human interaction with humanoid robots. On the one hand, robust techniques are researched that recognize emotional states from multi-sensory input, such as facial expressions, gestures and speech. On the other hand, mechanisms are under development that generate and display emotional states of robots, for example, by deformations of synthetic skin. In my talk, I will describe various computational approaches to implement empathic behaviors in a robot. Besides analytic approaches that are informed by theories from the cognitive and social sciences, I will discuss empirical approaches that enable a robot to learn empathic behaviors from recordings of human-human interactions or from life interactions with human interlocutors.

Contents

Transparency as an Ethical Safeguard

Anna Spagnolli[1(✉)], Lily E. Frank[2], Pim Haselager[3],
and David Kirsh[4]

[1] Department of General Psychology, Human Inspired Technologies
Research Centre, Padua University, Padua, Italy
anna.spagnolli@unipd.it
[2] Technical University of Eindhoven, Eindhoven, The Netherlands
L.E.Frank@tue.nl
[3] Donders Institute for Brain, Cognition and Behaviour,
Radboud University, Nijmegen, The Netherlands
w.haselager@donders.ru.nl
[4] University of California at San Diego, La Jolla, USA
kirsh@ucsd.edu

Abstract. Transparency seems to represent a solution to many ethic issues generated by systems that collect implicit data from users to model the user themselves based on programmed criteria. However, making such systems transparent – besides being a major technical challenge - risks raising more issues than it solves, actually reducing the user's ability to protect themselves while trying to put them in control. Are transparent systems only a chimera, which provides a seemingly useful information *pastiche* while failing to make sense upon closer examination? Scholars from ethics and cognitive science share their thoughts on how to achieve genuine transparency and the value of transparency.

Keywords: Symbiotic system · Ethics · Transparency · Implicit data

1 Transparency in Symbiotic Systems

In Human-Computer Interaction a system is considered transparent when it disappears, i.e. when it requires no specific attention from the user and leaves users free to engage in their activity. The system acquires center stage only if some problems emerge with the interpretation of its affordances and functions, an event which is considered to derive from bad design and which should be prevented as much as possible [4]. In the context of the ethics of technology, the transparency of a technology, by contrast, does not exclude the user from focusing attention on the tool, and its aim is not to facilitate performance by user or tool. Here, transparency refers to the extent to which the system discloses criteria of its functioning [3]. The goal of transparency in the context of ethics is not to enable users to effectively and easily operate a given device, it is to enable them to use such a device responsibly. The metaphor for transparency in this sense is the 'why-did-you-do-that?' button: the systems must disclose the criteria, sources, and rationales leading to its output as a way to make sure that no bias is introduced into the

J. Ham et al. (Eds.): Symbiotic 2017, LNCS 10727, pp. 1–6, 2018.
https://doi.org/10.1007/978-3-319-91593-7_1

process and to ensure that users are in a position to make informed decisions about input – giving data to the system and about output – using what the system in turn gives back.

Transparency has increasingly become the focus of many initiatives trying to deal with the ethical issues raised by systems that make decisions for us autonomously, such as those developed by Artificial Intelligence (AI), and especially those that are fed with personal information implicitly remitted to them, as is the case in what we call symbiotic systems [2]. In both these instances, transparency seems to be a critical safeguard protecting the user from unethical exploitation of their data and reducing the chance of unforeseen unethical actions resulting from system output.

There is growing appreciation that such systems must be regulated and that public bodies and professional associations must assume responsibility for such regulation. This task has been taken up by large international bodies such as, for instance, the EU in its General Data Protection Regulation, in particular Articles 12 and 13[1] or by self-regulatory guidelines from professional associations, such as the 'Ethically aligned design' guidelines by IEEE standard[2] and the Statement on Algorithmic Transparency and Accountability by ACM[3]. The idea that transparency, in its ethical sense, is one of the main safeguards of users' rights when dealing with personal data-processing technologies is dominant in all these regulations, principles and recommendations.

These efforts face several challenges. From the technical perspective, AI might work "without clear mappings to chains of inference that are easy for a human to understand" (see footnote 1); from a market perspective, a company might want to protect its own algorithms from being revealed to defend its competitiveness; from a psychological perspective, the user might be overwhelmed by information that s/he cannot manage. The very metaphor of a "why-did-you-do-that?" button is tricky. Why would a user know when a decision was or will be potentially risky? How might a user know when to press the button, or know when it is relevant to check the rationale behind the systems' output in order to make responsible decisions about it?

Identifying the challenges to genuine transparency from the user's perspective and ways to deal with these challenges was the topic of one ethical panel at Symbiotic 2017. Two scholars of ethics, Lily E. Frank (Technical University of Eindhoven) and Pim Haselager (Donders Institute for Brain, Cognition and Behaviour, Radboud University, Nijmegen) and one scholar of cognitive science, David Kirsh (Department of Cognitive Science UCSD & Leverhulme Visiting Professor Bartlett School of Architecture, University College London) have kindly accepted to share their thoughts about this topic. Anna Spagnolli organized and chaired the panel. The following is a synthesis approved by all authors.

---

[1] http://eur-lex.europa.eu/legal-content/EN/TXT/PDF/?uri=CELEX:32016R0679.

[2] http://standards.ieee.org/develop/indconn/ec/autonomous_systems.html.

[3] https://www.acm.org/binaries/content/assets/publicpolicy/2017_usacm_statement_algorithms.pdf.

2 What Would Ensure Genuine Transparency to Users? Panelists' Remarks

2.1 Pim Haselager: Want to Know vs. Ought to Know

I see an important aspect of transparency as being aware of what falls under one's control. I think this has two different meanings: what one wants to know and what one needs to know. The former refers to knowing what happens to my data or why the algorithm came up with a given decision. My primary example of a transparent tool in this sense would be to endow a system with some straightforward, self-explanatory system, the way a hammer's affordances are grasped. For me, the notion of affordance seems useful because it fits nicely with the non-inferential directness aimed for by symbiotic systems. The latter meaning of transparency is less discussed; it pertains to *transparency as the awareness of information required to use a system responsibly.* I make a plea that people get some sort of 'license' (not unlike a driver's license) before being allowed to use autonomous systems. You cannot simply not use certain technologies without having a reasonable understanding -on the basis of what you need to know about it- in order to deal adequately with them, make morally responsible decisions while using them and avoid e.g. negligence. What this means in practice will vary in different areas (like driving lessons vary for cars or motor cycles), for instance robotics, neurotechnology and algorithmic decision-making, and most likely also in different subareas.

2.2 Lily Frank: Transparency vs. Trust

Transparency has to do with making information available to a public or set of users regarding a particular system, but what remains vague is the quality of information to be revealed in order for a system to be considered transparent, the extent of information revealed, and level of understandability of that information. Most importantly, whether or not access to it will enable and support people to make decisions consistent with their value and priorities. I think that one the final goals of transparency should be to *expose the possible risks the user is taking and reveal the power imbalances* that already exist or are being created between the user and other institutions by use of the technology. Consequently, I see that in addition to transparency the user needs to be able trust that system. The direct link between trust and transparency should be less confidently assumed. *Trust, unlike transparency alone, includes the more general set of beliefs that the system will act in my best interests or at least consistently with my best interests or protecting my interests in a particular domain.* We should remain cautious about the burden of moral work that a concept like transparency can perform.

2.3 David Kirsh: Some Predictions About Solutions

Imagine an implant that tracks glucose levels and insulin, while also sensing and recording activity level and food consumption. To know what a person has eaten smart glasses or soon smart contact lenses would observe food choices. It's extra feature is that it can recommend items on a restaurant menu, or suggest food options from among the possibilities in the visual field by tagging visual input. Such a device knows a tremendous about its wearer. How can someone decide whether their privacy is being breached, as in the film Being John Malkovich? How can they know what their data is worth to the corporate owners of the product? How can they know whether there are alliances or back end deals that give rise to manipulative recommendations when there is no dietary reason to prefer food A to B?

Given the closely coupled connection between device and human this implantable service might qualify as an example of extended mind. It extends the boundaries of mind to glucose and insulin monitoring, and it encodes in vision analytics of activity and person specific consequences of food choice. All in real-time. Once a person habituates to it, it becomes a part of the person: if someone else were to take it off without permission, they would commit assault and battery. It is more than just property they own.

This mind extender is one of thousands that will soon be part of our augmented selves. We will need tools to ensure that we know what is going on because of the constant threat of parasitism. This raises huge questions for law, economics and ethics.

To deal with the transparency issue one easy to imagine solution is to create *smart contracts* that provide users with fair access to those pieces of their extended mind that others are more in control of. In particular, a smart contract would allow a user, if they so wished, to follow the distribution of their personal information as it metastasizes across companies and aggregators. Who sells or shares it with whom and for what? Once information is sold by the original company what can it be used for by others? What kind of momentary payoffs, communication with third parties take place?

A smart contract is inspired by the block-chain security model, where the provenance of goods and information is kept track of as it is transferred from hand to hand. The same model could be used to track the propagation of information across services and entities of various sorts, allowing the person whose data is being shared to ask, at any moment, questions about who is receiving and using their data. This promises to partially rebalance the current information asymmetry (see Kirsh in [3]), because without such intelligible feedback only the seller of the information knows what they are collecting, how it might be used, what it is worth. The person whose information it is (or should be) knows none of these things. They are exposed and in constant danger of exploitation.

With tracking comes the possibility of a new market for bots whose job is to calculate the risk of privacy loss, the value of information, and the danger of excessive trust. Another possibility is that our own agent bots might sell our information for us. This last idea means that with smart contracting there may be new markets for buying and selling personal information and for setting smart perimeters on how far one's information can be propagated and with what risk. This is a far cry from simple transparency, for now we must trust AI agents who will act on our behalf, watching for risk in its many forms. It is our AI guardian and agent who sees the value, risk and data being collected, not us.

3   What's Next?

As Turilli and Floridi pinpoint, transparency is not yet a full-fledged ethical principle [6]; it is instead an enabling principle for successfully fulfilling some ethical principles, which might be – for instance - protecting privacy. What has been described in this panel report illustrates some strategies though which transparency may become 'enabling' to the user: the provided information must be understood by the user, limited in amount to what is necessary to make a decision and well connected to the users' goals, priorities and responsibilities. This we have considered as a genuine, *bona fide* form of transparency different from a façade transparency set up by a service provider to formally fulfill some legal obligations to be transparent. But even when it is genuine, transparency might not protect the user as much as one would expect. Acquisti et al. describe two risks deriving from making a system transparent to the user: the control paradox and the user's (unnecessary) responsibilization [1]. The former resides in users taking more risks with a transparent system because they feel they are more in control than in opaque cases. The latter consists of shifting the responsibility from the system to the user.

There is clearly much work to be done to make symbiotic systems genuinely transparent and for transparency to be ethically enabling, rather than just making some system information public. The panel goal was to pinpoint the need for work in symbiotic systems. Some additional insights partially related to transparency can be found in the papers selected for this volume from Ruijten et al., and from Gamberini et al. We otherwise refer the reader to some projects that set transparency within their main goals: the Trust and Transparency project at the Leverhulme Center for the Future of Intelligence[4]; the Global Summit on AI for Good organized by the United Nation agency specialized agency International Telecommunication Union[5]; the Partnership on IA between Amazon, Google, IBM, Microsoft, Facebook and other key players having fair, transparent and accountable Artificial Intelligence as one of its thematic pillars[6]; OPEN AI, co-chaired by Sam Altman and Elon Musk and committed to only develop safe AI solutions; and recently funded EU projects such as Types[7] and Privacy Flag[8].

References

1. Acquisti, A., Adjerid, I., Brandimarte, L.: Gone in 15 seconds: the limits of privacy transparency and control. IEEE Secur. Priv. **11**(4), 72–74 (2013)

---

[4] http://lcfi.ac.uk/projects/trust-and-transparency/.

[5] https://www.itu.int/en/ITU-T/AI/Pages/201706-default.aspx.

[6] https://www.partnershiponai.org/thematic-pillars/.

[7] http://www.types-project.eu/.

[8] http://privacyflag.eu/.

2. Gamberini, L., Spagnolli, A.: Towards a definition of symbiotic relations between humans and machines. In: Gamberini, L., Spagnolli, A., Jacucci, G., Blankertz, B., Freeman, J. (eds.) Symbiotic 2016. LNCS, vol. 9961, pp. 1–4. Springer, Cham (2017). https://doi.org/10.1007/978-3-319-57753-1_1
3. The IEEE Global Initiative on Ethics of Autonomous and Intelligent Systems. Ethically Aligned Design: A Vision for Prioritizing Human Well-being with Autonomous and Intelligent Systems, Version 2. IEEE (2017). http://standards.ieee.org/develop/indconn/ec/autonomous_systems.html
4. Norman, D.: The Design of Everyday Things: Revised and Expanded Edition. Basic Books, New York (2013)
5. Spagnolli, A., Conti, M., Guerra, G., Freeman, J., Kirsh, D., van Wynsberghe, A.: Adapting the system to users based on implicit data: ethical risks and possible solutions. In: Gamberini, L., Spagnolli, A., Jacucci, G., Blankertz, B., Freeman, J. (eds.) Symbiotic 2016. LNCS, vol. 9961, pp. 5–22. Springer, Cham (2017). https://doi.org/10.1007/978-3-319-57753-1_2
6. Turilli, M., Floridi, L.: The ethics of information transparency. Ethics Inf. Technol. **11**(2), 105–112 (2009)

A Comparison of Different Electrodermal Variables in Response to an Acute Social Stressor

Anne-Marie Brouwer[1]([✉]), Maurice van Beurden[1], Lars Nijboer[2],
Luc Derikx[2], Olaf Binsch[1], Christa Gjaltema[1],
and Matthijs Noordzij[2,3]

[1] TNO Human Factors, Soesterberg, The Netherlands
anne-marie.brouwer@tno.nl
[2] Department of Cognitive Psychology and Ergonomics,
Universtiy of Twente, Enschede, The Netherlands
[3] Department of Psychology, Health, and Technology,
Universtiy of Twente, Enschede, The Netherlands

Abstract. We investigated electrodermal activity (EDA) in 130 participants undergoing a shortened version of a novel easy, effective and controlled method to induce stress (the Sing-a-Song Stress Test). We compared skin conductance level (SCL), amplitude and number of skin conductance response peaks with respect to their sensitivity to the known stressor, for different scenarios of interests. EDA increased after stressor-onset for almost all participants. At a group level, the three variables were about equally sensitive. When examining the increase following the stressor with respect to preceding EDA within one individual, peak amplitude was most sensitive. Peak measures were clearly most sensitive in a simulated between-subject scenario (i.e., testing the difference in EDA between stress and non-stress intervals as if data originated from different, stressed and non-stressed groups of individuals). Peaks can be extracted by continuous decomposition (CDA) or through-to-peak analysis (TTP). In all analyses performed, CDA outperformed TTP. We thus recommend CDA peak amplitude for monitoring physiological stress effects in e.g. symbiotic systems.

Keywords: Electrodermal activity · GSR · Skin conductance · Stress
Arousal · Stress induction · Sing-a-Song Stress Test

1 Introduction

The ability to cope with high levels of emotional, cognitive and physiological stress is an important skill for many professionals, such as soldiers or police officers, since they operate in complex and highly demanding environments. The current developments in gaming and simulation technology and the miniaturization of sensor and monitoring technology offers an opportunity to develop new advanced training systems combining VR technology, serious gaming environments and physiological computing. There is increasing interest to use simulated environments to change the content based on the current individual stress experience. In symbiotic applications such as these, stress

© Springer International Publishing AG, part of Springer Nature 2018
J. Ham et al. (Eds.): Symbiotic 2017, LNCS 10727, pp. 7–17, 2018.
https://doi.org/10.1007/978-3-319-91593-7_2

should be estimated in individuals without needing to question them about their stress experience - individuals should not be distracted from the task they are performing. Another example where one is interested to monitor individuals continuously and study when a stress response occurs, and how strong this is, is monitoring phobic patients such that their treatment can be tailored [1]. A different type of scenario that benefits from implicit markers of stress are studies that evaluate the success of a stress resilience training (i.e., examining the stress response of a group of individuals that received training to that of a control group) or compare stress responses in other types of groups (e.g. pathological, or professional – [2]). This is especially important when dealing with populations who have difficulties to properly indicate their level of stress verbally, or are expected to show response bias when using questionnaires. In these examples, one would like to test the response to a known stressor between groups rather than responses within an individual. Finally, it may be of interest to know whether an individual is in a stressed state or not (e.g. a patient coming in for treatment). In this case, there is no individual baseline value or known stress response. In each case one might need a different set of evaluation criteria to predict the experienced stress of an individual.

Electrodermal activity (EDA), or changes in the electrical activity of the skin, has been recognized for decades to be a reliable marker of physiological arousal, which can be considered as an important component of stress. It is thought to reflect activity of the 'fight or flight' sympathetic branch of the autonomous nervous system [3, 4]. The physiological basis for EDA is not fully understood, but sweat gland activity is certainly implicated [5]. We here consider commonly used skin conductance variables that can be observed when applying an external source of current on the skin (i.e. exosomatic method), in contrast to only using skin potential (endosomatic method – [5]). Active sweat glands cause higher conductivity of current. To quantify this, different variables can be extracted from the raw signal: overall Skin Conductance Level (SCL) during a given period of time, and variables related to fast skin conductance changes (skin conductance responses, hereafter referred to as 'peaks'). Peak-related variables include the number of peaks and their mean amplitude during a given period in time. In order to detect these peaks, hand-extracted through-to-peak (TTP) methods have originally been used. These methods have later been automated by finding values exceeding certain thresholds [6]. Another approach (CDA-continuous decomposition analysis) that is less dependent on the individual shapes of the peaks was proposed by Benedek and Kaernbach [4]. Using deconvolution of the skin conductance signal, the tonic (SCL) and the phasic (skin conductance peak) activity can be recovered.

We here systematically compare the sensitivity of different electrodermal variables to a well-timed, acute social stressor that is controlled for body movements in a large number of participants. Many current methods that have been used to induce stress result in relatively modest physiological changes (e.g. [7, 8]) or are not controlled for body movements (which by themselves affect physiology) and are relatively cumbersome (e.g. [9]). In the current study, the presentation of the stressor follows a modified version of the 'Sing-a-Song Stress Test' (SSST) [10]. In the SSST, participants are presented with 9 'neutral' sentences, each followed by a countdown interval of 60 s. After that, a sentence is presented in which participants are asked to sing a song of their choice aloud after the end of the subsequent countdown interval during which participants sit still in the same way as before. This procedure leads to relatively strong increases in heart rate, skin conductance level and pupil size when comparing the countdown interval following the stress sentence to the one following the last neutral sentence [2, 10]. In the current study, we further shortened the stress induction procedure by using less sentences and intervals of 30 rather than 60 s. Also, the neutral sentences involved mental tasks. The original version of the SSST cannot differentiate between effects of cognitive mental processes (associated with task difficulty, which has been shown to increase of electrodermal activity – [11]) and effects of affective processes. Using sentences that ask participants to perform cognitive tasks rather than have them only read a sentence is an attempt to somewhat rectify the difference in cognitive load between the stress sentence (leading participants to think of a song they would want to sing) and the neutral sentences. Finally, the current version of the SSST features one rather than two individuals as audience for the singing. Taken together, this new, shortened version, requiring less people, can be finished under ten minutes. This makes it a very fast and low demand social stress alternative for the well-known and effective, but more cumbersome Trier Social Stress Test [9].

The sensitivity of electrodermal variables to a stressor can be defined for a whole group (where a high sensitivity indicates that all recorded individuals show a large increase of electrodermal activity in response to the stressor) or for an individual (where a high sensitivity indicates that the increase of electrodermal activity in response to the stressor is high compared to the variability in electrodermal activity of that individual in the preceding time interval). In addition, we can view effects of a stressor as a state, i.e. without making use of the electrodermal baseline of the individual. In that case, a sensitive electrodermal variable as recorded after a stressor displays high values relative to the mean and the variation of measurements in a baseline situation. These three types of sensitivity map onto the three groups of examples mentioned at the start of the introduction. The stress response in a group is important for comparing different groups; the stress response within an individual relative to a longer preceding interval is important for adaptive automation such as adapting gaming content to an individual's state; the stress state without knowing a personal baseline is important for applications in which the question is whether newly observed individuals are in a state of more or less stress. We compare the sensitivity of SCL, peak amplitude and number of peaks (where the latter two variables are extracted using CDA or (automatic) TTP) under each of these three scenarios.

2 Methods

2.1 Participants

154 participants (mostly college students participating for course credit) took part in the experiment. As recommended [6], visual checks were performed on plots of skin conductance data to identify failed measurements, "non-responding" individuals (indicated by an absence of peaks in a given measurement) or incorrect classification of peaks. Data from these problematic measurements as well as data in which other technical problems occurred during measurement were removed from further analysis.

After this quality control step data from 130 participants remained. Mean age was 22 years (std = 3.4, range = 18–42) and 85 were female. Participants were told that the experiment was about personality and fitness and were debriefed about the real purpose afterwards. The study was approved by the ethics committee of the University of Twente. All participants signed an informed consent in accordance with the Declaration of Helsinki, stressing the right to quit participation at any time.

2.2 Materials

Electrodermal activity was measured with two skin conductance sensors from the Biograph infiniti package (Bio-Medical instruments, Clinton Township, MI, USA). The skin conductance sensors were placed on the ventral side of the medial phalanges of the ring and index finger at the left hand and kept in place with Velcro straps. Recording frequency was 256 Hz and sensor supply voltage was 7.3 mV.

2.3 Design and Procedure

After signing the informed consent form, the participant was seated behind a laptop to fill out two questionnaires with demographical and personality questions (not analyzed here). After the participant finished the questionnaires, the experimenter invited a confederate in the room as a second participant whose turn it would be next. The confederate was seated behind the laptop (supposedly to fill out the questionnaires as well) while the participant was relocated in the same room to sit approximately 60 cm in front of a 1280 × 720 60 Hz flat screen with the experimental stimuli. Sensors to measure skin conductance and heart rate (not analyzed here) were attached. Participants were asked to move as little as possible and follow the instructions on the screen that were exchanged with a counter counting down until the next instruction. (See for the exact instructions Table 1). Participants were first instructed to sit calm and relax

Table 1. Instructions translated into English and the duration of the subsequent countdown interval.

	Instruction	Duration (s)
Baseline 1/4	Sit calm, try to relax and focus on your breathing while watching the counter counting down	120
Neutral 1	Think of animals starting with the letter P	30
Neutral 2	Think of objects one can find in a kitchen	30
Neutral 3	Think of the necessary items when organizing a wedding	30
Neutral 4	Think of as many team sports practiced without a ball as possible	30
Preparing	The next assignment will be to sing a song aloud – think about songs to sing for the next 30 s	30
Singing	Now sing a song for 30 s aloud and try to keep your arms still. Keep singing!	30
Baseline 5/8	Sit calm, try to relax and focus on your breathing while watching the counter counting down	120

for 2 min. Then four times an instruction to perform a simple cognitive task was displayed for 5 s, each time followed by a countdown interval in which a number on the screen counted from 30 to 1. Then the sing-a-song stress sentence was presented, telling the participants that they would be instructed to sing after the countdown interval had ended. In the subsequent singing instruction, participants were asked to sing for 30 s. When participants stopped singing, the experimenter indicated that they should continue singing, until 30 s had passed and the screen instructed them to relax for another 2 min.

Before and after the SSST, participants were asked to fill out Likert scales on experienced stress (not analyzed here). During the experiment, the experimenter stayed in the room.

2.4 Data Analysis

Skin conductance data were down sampled to 16 Hz, and processed with Continuous Decomposition Analysis (CDA) as implemented in Ledalab [4]. The peak (phasic) activity was also calculated using Ledalab's Through-to-Peak analysis (TTP). The threshold for peak amplitude was set at .03 μs [6]. CDA skin conductance level (SCL), CDA/TTP mean peak amplitude and CDA/TTP number of peaks were determined for each participant and each of the following 30-s time segments: baseline interval 1 through 4, countdown interval following neutral sentence 1 through 4, countdown interval following the stress sentence in which participants prepared to sing, singing interval and baseline intervals 5 through 8.

The main parameter of interest for all electrodermal variables is the 'stress response' that we define as the value during the stress countdown interval (preparation) minus the value during preceding countdown interval (following the fourth neutral sentence) separately for each participant. Experienced stress may actually be higher during singing itself, but during this interval electrodermal activity will also be affected by speech and other movements of the body.

3 Results

3.1 Stress Response in the Group

Figure 1 through Fig. 3 show respectively SCL, peak amplitude (as determined using (a) CDA and (b) TTP) and number of peaks (as determined using (a) CDA and (b) TTP) in the 14 subsequent 30-s time segments, averaged across participants. All variables show an effect of the stressor: values are higher during the stress countdown interval (preparation) compared to the previous countdown interval (neutral 4). Figure 4 shows density plots of the stress responses (the difference between preparation and neutral 4) for all variables. Results of Wilcoxon signed rank tests on stress responses are given in Table 2. Stress responses are significantly larger than zero for all measures, with all z-scores exceeding 7.4. Note that the error bars (standard deviations) and violins in Fig. 1 through Fig. 3 convey information about the variation in the overall values

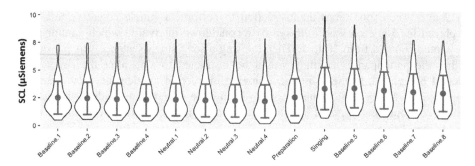

Fig. 1. SCL in the 14 subsequent 30-s time segments, averaged across participants. Error bars represent standard deviations.

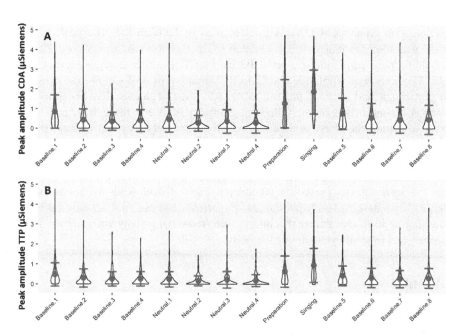

Fig. 2. Peak amplitude (as determined using (a) CDA and (b) TTP) in the 14 subsequent 30-s time segments, averaged across participants. Error bars represent standard deviations.

between participants. This variation somewhat masks the fact that the increase in value from neutral 4 to preparation is very consistent: 90% of participants showed an increase in SCL, 95% in peak amplitude CDA, 89% in peak amplitude TTP, 97% in number of peaks CDA and 96% in number of peaks TTP.

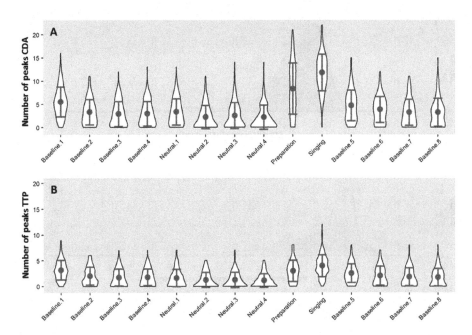

Fig. 3. Number of peaks (as determined using (a) CDA and (b) TTP) in the 14 subsequent 30-s time segments, averaged across participants. Error bars represent standard deviations.

3.2 Stress Response Within an Individual Relative to a Longer Preceding Interval

To determine the sensitivity of electrodermal variables to the stressor within an individual over a longer period of time, we computed an effect size for each variable and each participant by dividing the stress response by the standard deviation of the values of the preceding seven 30-s segments. A high value indicates that an individual's increase of electrodermal activity in response to the stressor is high compared to the individual's natural variability in electrodermal activity in the preceding time intervals. Table 3 presents the mean, standard deviation and range of the individual effect sizes.

Within paired non-parametric tests (Wilcoxon signed rank) on the effect sizes show that the effect size of number of peaks CDA is significantly larger than that of TTP; and that the effect size of peak amplitude CDA is significantly larger than that of TTP. In fact, the effect size of peak amplitude CDA is larger than that of all other measures (all p-values < .01).

3.3 Stressed Versus Non-stressed State Between Two Virtual Groups of Participants

To determine the sensitivity of electrodermal variables to identify whether an individual is in a stressed state, i.e. without knowing his or her baseline, we compared values recorded in the stress countdown interval to values recorded in the preceding countdown interval as if they were coming from two groups of people; a stressed and a

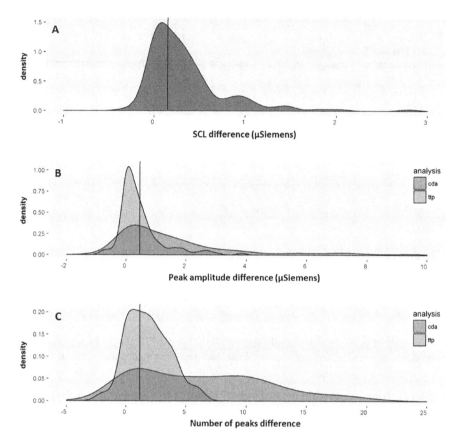

Fig. 4. Density plots of stress responses SCL (A), peak amplitude as extracted through CDA and TTP (B), and number of peaks as extracted through CDA and TTP (C).

Table 2. Results of Wilcoxon signed rank tests on stress responses

	p-value	Signed rank	z-value
SCL	9.985E−20	8169	9.0891
Peak amplitude CDA	2.125E−19	6763	9.0066
Peak amplitude TTP	7.458E−14	6108	7.4796
Number of peaks CDA	1.617E−18	6283	8.7813
Number of peaks TTP	1.633E−16	4993	8.2464

relaxed group (using an independent samples non-parametric test: Wilcoxon rank sum). Not unexpected due to the large variability in SCL baseline between participants, the test on SCL did not reach significance. For all other variables, there was a significant effect (see Table 4).

Table 3. Mean, standard deviation and range of the effect sizes of individual participants

	Mean effect size	Stdev	Range
SCL	2.7419	2.9923	−0.250–5.734
Peak amplitude CDA	6.8739	10.006	−3.132–16.880
Peak amplitude TTP	3.9444	7.230	−3.285–11.174
Number of peaks CDA	4.0635	4.760	−0.696–8.823
Number of peaks TTP	1.8783	2.065	−0.18–3.944

Table 4. Results of Wilcoxon rank sum tests comparing stress countdown intervals to preceding countdown in an unpaired fashion.

	p-value	Signed rank	z-value
SCL	0.057	1903	1.8120
Peak amplitude CDA	5.870E−18	8635	2.2177
Peak amplitude TTP	2.398E−12	7009	2.1172
Number of peaks CDA	3.043E−20	9217	2.2510
Number of peaks TTP	1.344E−14	7702	2.1547

4 Discussion

The simplified and further controlled version of the SSST elicits clear electrodermal stress responses. For almost all participants, higher electrodermal activity was found after presentation of the stress sentence, where this is not due to motor behavior because people are only preparing to sing and do not actually sing or move yet [10]. This further supports the Sing-a-Song Stress Test as a valuable standardized, quick and easy to apply stress induction method. The cognitive tasks as used in this version of the SSST, and the presumed associated arousal, did not result in a noticeable increase of electrodermal activity as indicated by Figs. 1, 2 and 3 (no higher values for the neutral countdown intervals compared to the first four resting baseline segments). Potential subtle effects may have been masked by the observed trend of electrodermal activity to decrease over time.

With respect to sensitivity of the peak variables, CDA outperforms TTP, both for amplitude and number of peaks. This holds true for all three scenarios (overall stress response in a group; stress response within an individual as compared to her or his variability in preceding electrodermal activity over a longer interval; differences between stressed and non-stressed individuals). This is indicated by the finding that z-values always tended to be higher when peak variables were determined using CDA compared to TTP (Tables 2 and 4) and that effect sizes are significantly larger when peak variables were determined using CDA compared to TTP (Table 3). Figures 2 and 3 show that compared to TTP, CDA captures higher values of peak amplitude and (especially) higher number of peaks. The higher sensitivity of CDA for the SSST stressor corroborates findings indicating higher sensitivity for CDA for a short event-related noise paradigm [4].

SCL shows large variation between participants relative to the average increase in SCL due to the stressor (Fig. 1). However, the Wilcoxon signed rank test in Sect. 3.1 shows that the SCL stress response (i.e., the increase of SCL after presentation of the stress sentence compared to the previous count down interval) is comparable, and even tends to be strongest, to the stress response for the peak measures. When examining electrodermal activity over time within a single participant (effect size in Sect. 3.2), SCL is less sensitive compared to the CDA peak measures. Thus, SCL seems to be a relatively variable signal when viewed over a longer time before the stressor. In accordance with this, Fig. 1 shows that at the start of the measurements, SCL is almost at the level of the stress countdown interval. This also holds for number of peaks TTP which accordingly shows the lowest effect size. Peak amplitude CDA looks most stable across the preceding intervals, and also captures some very strong positive responses (see range indicated in Table 3).

When comparing SCL values in the stress 'preparation' interval to the values as recorded during the preceding countdown interval using a test for independent samples (i.e. treating the data as coming from two groups of individuals; a stressed and a relaxed group), the difference in SCL did not reach significance. This means that when the baseline value of an individual is not known, SCL is not suitable to estimate whether an individual is stressed. Consistent with this, Hogervorst et al. [12] found that a measure reflecting SCL did not distinguish between individuals who were about to undergo stressful eye laser surgery, while heart rate related variables did. The other, peak-related variables showed a clearly significant effect (Table 4), indicating that these can be used when the baseline of an individual is unknown.

Overall, our results show CDA peak amplitude to be the most stable indicator of the occurrence of the stressor across scenarios. SCL is an effective measure when a comparison with an individual's immediately preceding baseline is available. If this baseline is not available, SCL is clearly less useful whereas the peak measures (amplitude and number, especially when determined using CDA) still are reliable indicators of stress.

We conclude this paper by pointing out some observations and directions for future research.

All electrodermal variables show higher values during the singing itself compared to the countdown interval before. This could be due to a combination of stronger mental arousal (e.g. the singing itself is scarier than preparing for it), body movement (most notably speech and breathing) and delayed effects of the end of the countdown interval preceding the singing (which may have been most arousing). It would be of interest to tease these factors somewhat apart in future research and analyses.

By specifying the time that participants should sing followed by a resting baseline, the used version of the SSST is also suitable to examine recovery processes. Figure 1 through Fig. 3 suggests an essential distinction between SCL and peak variables: while all variables show a decrease in electrodermal activity, this seems to occur at a much slower pace for SCL compared to the peak variables.

Acknowledgement. We are grateful to Imke Silderhuis, Sacha Jenderny, Steven de Vries, and Laura Duddeck for data collection and preparing the experiment, and Maarten Hogervorst for helpful discussions on this paper. The present study was partially funded by the defense program V1532 AMPERE.

References

1. Rizzo, A., Graap, K., Mclay, R.N., Perlma, K., Rothbaum, B.O., Reger, G., Parsons, T., Difede, J., Pair, J., et al.: Virtual Iraq: initial case reports from a VR exposure therapy application for combat-related post traumatic stress disorder. In: Proceedings of the International Workshop on Virtual Rehabilitation, pp. 124–130. IEEE Press, Washington (2007)
2. Toet, A., Bijlsma, M., Brouwer, A.-M.: Stress response and facial trustworthiness judgements in civilians and military. SAGE Open **7**(3), 1–11 (2017). http://journals.sagepub.com/doi/full/10.1177/2158244017725386
3. Dawson, M.E., Schell, A.M., Filion, D.L.: The electrodermal system. In: Cacioppo, J.T., Tassinary, L.G., Berntson, G.G. (eds.) Handbook of Psychophysiology. Cambridge University Press, Cambridge (2007)
4. Benedek, M., Kaernbach, C.: A continuous measure of phasic electrodermal activity. J. Neurosci. Methods **190**(1), 80–91 (2010)
5. Andreassi, J.L.: Psychophysiology: Human Behavior and Physiological Response, 5th edn. Psychology Press, Taylor & Francis Group, LLC, New York (2007)
6. Boucsein, W.: Electrodermal Activity, 2nd edn. Springer, New York (2012). https://doi.org/10.1007/978-1-4614-1126-0
7. Eisenberg, N., Fabes, R.A., Bustamante, D., Mathy, R.M., Miller, P.A., Lindholm, E.: Differentiation of vicariously induced emotional reactions in children. Dev. Psychol. **24**, 237–246 (1988)
8. Lang, P.J., Bradley, M.M., Cuthbert, B.N.: International Affective Picture System (IAPS): affective ratings of pictures and instruction manual. Technical report, University of Florida, Gainesville, Fl (2005)
9. Kirschbaum, C., Pirke, K.M., Hellhammer, D.H.: The "Trier Social Stress Test"—a tool for investigating psychobiological stress responses in a laboratory setting. Neuropsychobiology **28**, 76–78 (1993)
10. Brouwer, A.-M., Hogervorst, M.A.: A new paradigm to induce mental stress: the Sing-a-Song Stress Test (SSST). Front. Neurosci. **8**, 224 (2014)
11. Brouwer, A.-M., Hogervorst, M.A., Holewijn, M., van Erp, J.B.F.: Evidence for effects of task difficulty but not learning on neurophysiological variables associated with effort. Int. J. Psychophysiol. **93**, 242–252 (2014)
12. Hogervorst, M.A., Brouwer, A.-M., Vos, W.: Physiological correlates of stress in individuals about to undergo eye laser surgery. In: Humaine Association Conference on Affective Computing and Intelligent Interaction, pp. 473–478. IEEE Computer Society (2013)

Monitoring Mental State During Real Life Office Work

Anne-Marie Brouwer[(✉)], Loïs van de Water, Maarten Hogervorst,
Wessel Kraaij, Jan Maarten Schraagen, and Koen Hogenelst

TNO, The Hague, The Netherlands
anne-marie.brouwer@tno.nl

Abstract. Monitoring an individual's mental state using unobtrusively measured signals is regarded as an essential element in symbiotic human-machine systems. However, it is not straightforward to model the relation between mental state and such signals in real life, without resorting to (unnatural) emotion induction. We recorded heart rate, facial expression and computer activity of nineteen participants while working at the computer for ten days. In order to obtain 'ground truth' emotional state, participants indicated their current emotion using a valence-arousal affect grid every 15 min. We found associations between valence/arousal and the unobtrusively measured variables. There was some first success to predict subjective valence/arousal using personal classification models. Thus, real-life office emotions appear to vary enough, and can be reported well enough, to uncover relations with unobtrusively measured variables. This is required to be able to monitor individuals in real life more fine-grained than the frequency with which emotion is probed.

Keywords: Emotion · Affective computing · Heart rate · Facial expression
Ecological Momentary Assessment · Experience sampling · Privacy

1 Introduction

Human-machine interaction could benefit from continuous information about an individual user's affective or cognitive state that is extracted from the user in an implicit, unobtrusive way, i.e. without requiring him or her to repeatedly provide self-reports. Especially automated, 'smart' systems that aim to support the user could use this information to optimize support in real time (adaptive automation – [1] or symbiotic systems). In an offline fashion, such information could be used to evaluate the interaction between (certain types of) users with (certain types of) systems. An example is examining mental effort in novices and experts working with information presented through different types of display designs. Other potential applications of continuous mental state monitoring are in the health domain: continuous information about an employee's state may lead to timely detection of increased workload or stress levels, allowing for adaptive interventions to promote a healthier working environment. Traditional ways to probe individuals' mental state such as self-report questionnaires, (neuro)psychological tests, or neuroimaging tools, often provide only snapshots of information, are burdensome, time-consuming, and/or obtrusive. Technological

© Springer International Publishing AG, part of Springer Nature 2018
J. Ham et al. (Eds.): Symbiotic 2017, LNCS 10727, pp. 18–29, 2018.
https://doi.org/10.1007/978-3-319-91593-7_3

advances now allow us to record, store and process a multitude of physiological and behavioral data from individuals in their daily environment [2–4]. Examples of such data are movements as recorded by a wristband, activity using a GPS system, heart rate and features related to facial expression from camera images. All of these techniques may allow us to monitor individuals' physiological and physical state continuously, implicitly and unobtrusively and, on the basis of those data, allow us to make inferences on individuals' mental state.

We here focus on mental state in an office situation. Previous studies in the laboratory (including simulated office environments) showed that a range of variables can be used to distinguish between different levels of induced stress or workload (e.g. [5–7]). However, it is not known whether naturally occurring stress, in a real life office environment, can also be detected implicitly and unobtrusively [8]. We do not know of any study in a real-life office situation in which an individual's emotional state is estimated and validated continuously using continuous, implicit, and unobtrusive sources of information.

There are several challenges in the topic of monitoring an individual's emotion continuously and implicitly in real life. Sensors can be affected by noise from the environment at unknown times and in unknown ways. There is no known mapping of variables to emotion that holds across changing contexts. In real life, context changes all the time - people perform different activities which go together with different types of noise and different types of valuable information. In addition, relations between implicitly measured variables and mental state differ between individuals [5, 9]. Arguably, strong, invariant associations are not expected since physiology and behavior are not there to inform researchers about emotion, but reflect processes that help the individual interact with and survive in the world. A final and important challenge we want to stress is that especially when one wants to refrain from experimentally inducing emotions, it is difficult to obtain ground truth ('true') emotion as experienced in real life while this information is essential to train and validate models that infer emotions from variables.

In order to meet these challenges to the largest extent possible, we designed our real-life office study so as to potentially enable personalized models by obtaining a relatively large number of ground truth emotion labels. A large number of labels would also help to capture potentially small variations in (real life) emotions. An office study forms a good case for mental state monitoring research in general since the amount and severity of sensor noise and changes in context in an office situation is expected to be low compared to many other real life situations. Our approach is to follow a number of individuals doing their work at a computer in office rooms at our institute over 10 days, recording unobtrusive variables that may convey information about emotional state (heart rate, facial features and keyboard and mouse activity). In addition, the participants are asked to rate their current emotional state every 15 min. These ratings (approximately 290 per person) are treated as ground truth emotion. Repeatedly asking individuals to rate their current feelings is referred to as Ecological Momentary Assessment or experience sampling [10–12]. Experience sampling minimizes retrospective biases that may typically occur in longitudinal studies using questionnaires on few occasions [12, 13].

Our main research question is whether we can estimate emotion using unobtrusively measured variables in an office setting. In this case, this would be operationalized to predicting an individual's subjective rating using data that was collected implicitly in the minutes prior to this subjective rating. We present first results on this, but we also hope that the present paper can serve as an anchor point for designing other real-life (office) monitoring studies, given the scarcity of these studies in the literature which makes it difficult to estimate what can be asked of participants in terms of experience sampling and being monitored in general. While for research and monitoring purposes, large amounts of data are preferred, it is of the utmost importance that participants adhere to the instructions and do not drop out due to experienced obtrusiveness (having to answer questions repeatedly) or perceived violations of their privacy. Drop-out is a severe problem in real-life monitoring studies. We therefore report participants' study experiences, their thoughts regarding privacy, and their ideas towards real-life implementation. In addition, we describe how rated emotion varies during regular office work, where it is of interest to know whether it seems to vary enough to expect that modelling is ever possible. Finally, we present associations that we find between rated emotion and the different variables that were recorded, to give an impression of whether and how they are related and can be expected to be useful in a model for estimating emotion.

Implicit variables that may reflect emotional state during office work include a range of physiological variables, facial expression, body posture and computer interaction (e.g. [5, 8, 14, 15]). Based on considerations concerning ease of use, obtrusiveness and budget, we chose to include heart rate as recorded at the wrist, facial expression and computer interaction.

2   Methods

2.1   Participants

Nineteen participants were recruited by advertising within the participant pool of the Netherlands Organization for Applied Scientific Research (TNO), the community of the University of Utrecht and clients of certain thesis support companies. The mean age was 25.84 (SD = 4.78). Three participants quit after 5 days or less. The reasons for quitting communicated to the experimental leader were not related to the study itself (namely illness and job requirements). We analyzed data from the remaining 16 participants. All participants were students at the time of the experiment and working on their thesis or other study projects, which is what they were asked to do in the laboratory offices. Participants were not in a dependent relationship with any of the people involved in the research. They received €150 upon completion of the study. All participants were fully briefed beforehand as to what was expected of them and what was recorded. They signed an informed consent form in accordance with the Declaration of Helsinki. This study was approved by the TNO Institutional Review Board (TCPE).

2.2 Materials

Figure 1 shows two participants during the study (picture taken and used with their permission). For each participant, a personal work area was available which consisted of a desk, an adaptable chair, a Dell Windows 7 laptop on a laptop stand, a mouse, a keyboard and a USB hub. The laptops were provided by TNO and equipped with software required for the experiment and a webcam. A maximum of 5 participants worked in one of three office rooms that were dedicated to this study.

Fig. 1. Study environment.

Heart rate was recorded using a MIO Fuse heart rate wrist wearable. At every heartbeat the device sent a heartrate value to the local data server together with the wearable ID.

Computer activity was recorded using Noldus uLog keylogger (research Edition version 3.3). This program logged various parameters of keyboard usage and mouse usage, of which the number of keypresses per minute, the error-ratio (number of error keypresses (backspace and delete) in proportion to the total number of keypresses) and the number of application switches per minute were assessed in this study. To protect the participant's privacy, typed strings of text and names or content of documents, emails and websites were not recorded.

For measuring the participant's facial features, a webcam snapshot was taken every minute. These images were later analyzed using Noldus FaceReader 7.0. to extract different basic emotions and expression components, so-called action units [16]. The output of this software are scores for 20 different action units and eight basic emotions. We examined action units dimpler, lip corner puller, lid tightener, brow lowerer, outer brow raiser and inner brow raiser since earlier research suggested that these may contain information as to emotion in an office situation [5, 15]. We also examined the basic emotion outputs for disgusted, scared, surprised, angry, sad, happy and neutral.

Every 15 min a pop-up screen with an affect grid [17] appeared on the participant's computer screen. Figure 2 shows the version we used (translated from Dutch to English). Participants were instructed to indicate their current emotion by clicking the appropriate location in the grid, and subsequently click the 'ok' button. They could also click the pop-up away by clicking the 'ok' button immediately, but participants were asked to do this only when they really did not want to answer.

For investigating participants' overall experience as a participant in the study, including experienced obtrusiveness of the pop-up screen and privacy aspects, semi-structured one-to-one interviews were conducted at the end of the last working day. Open questions as well as Likert scale questions were used. The audio was recorded and notes were made by the experimental leader.

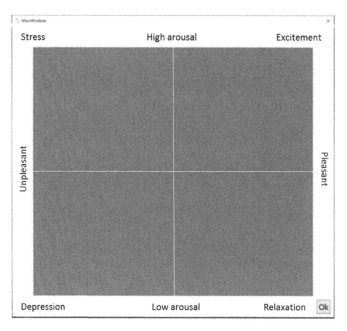

Fig. 2. Used pop-up affect grid (translated to English) for probing participants' current emotional state. Participants were instructed to indicate their current emotion by clicking the appropriate location in the grid, and subsequently click the 'ok' button.

2.3   Procedure

Most participants worked for 10 working days from 9:00 AM until 5:00 PM at the study location. The participation days were planned as consecutively as possible. One participant requested to join for longer than the 10 required days because of the pleasant working environment - she participated for 16 days. Another participant participated for 11 days to compensate for being absent due to appointments away from the study location. Each morning participants logged in on the study software with their participant ID and personal password. Then the heart rate wearable was placed on the participant's wrist and the connection with the local data server was checked. While participants were working, unobtrusive measurements were gathered and they were asked to rate their emotion every 15 min. Short individual breaks were allowed. In addition, each day at twelve o'clock all participants went to the canteen together for a lunch break. On their first participation day, participants received a short instruction about all measurements and they signed an informed consent form. Afterwards, two questionnaires were filled in (a personality questionnaire and a questionnaire on vitality: not analyzed here). At the end of each participation day, a short questionnaire was taken on global activities, emotion, stress and mental effort over the whole day (not analyzed here). On their last participation day, a one-to-one interview with the participant was conducted focused on their experience with the study obtrusiveness and privacy aspects.

2.4 Analysis

Some heart rate data were missing due to technical problems. This resulted in reduced datasets for four participants (6, 8, 9 days of data for three of the participants who had participated 10 days; and 14 days of data for the participant who joined the study for 16 days).

For each subjective rating, we determined an averaged value for each examined implicit measurement (heart rate, the thirteen facial expression features and four computer usage features) reflecting the 15 min interval preceding the time of rating. Spearman's correlation analyses were performed between these averaged values of each of the implicit measures, and valence and arousal scores on the other hand. This was done for each participant separately. The number of significant ($p < 0.05$) correlations as well as their direction of correlation were stored.

For classification, we trained linear SVM (Support Vector Machine) models for each participant to distinguish between the participant's highest and lowest 33% arousal scores, and between the participant's highest and lowest 33% valence scores. Included features were the averaged values for each examined implicit measurement (heart rate, facial expression features and computer usage features), except for the six action units since these did not appear to be informative from the correlation analyses. In order not to lose data points if there were missing data of one or some of the implicit measurements, missing values were replaced by mean values of the participant. Classification was performed using the Donders machine learning toolbox developed by [18] and implemented in the FieldTrip open source Matlab toolbox [19]. The features were standardized to have mean 0 and standard deviation 1 on the basis of data from the training set. We used 5-fold cross validation. For each participant, and each arousal and valence model, we determined whether classification was above chance using a binomial test. An alpha level of 5% was used.

3 Results

3.1 Ratings Affect Grid

Participants virtually never clicked the pop-up affect grid away without entering a location in the grid. Click locations in the affect grid suggested that none of the participants had aimed to click the same location - variability in ratings of naturally occurring emotions during office work seemed enough for further analysis. Figure 3 shows the responses of three different participants. They are the participant with the most dense cloud, with the widest cloud, and one of the approximately 7 participants who used the arousal in a more continuous way than valence – i.e. these participants tended to describe their emotion as either pleasant or unpleasant.

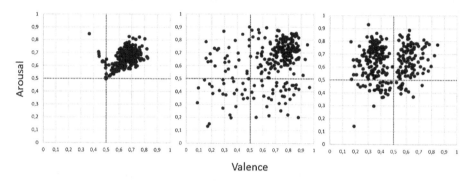

Fig. 3. Example data of three participants representing different types of response patterns. Each dot corresponds to one click in the affect grid – for each of the participants, all responses collected in the complete experiment are shown. See Fig. 2 for the lay-out of the grid as presented to the participants.

3.2   Correlation Analyses

Figure 4 shows the number of participants for whom we found significant correlation coefficients when checking correlations between reported emotions and implicit recordings, separately for the different pairs of variables and for the direction of correlation (negative or positive).

By chance, about 1 significant correlation (5% of 16) is expected for each pair. In general, computer activity, overall face expression (but not the independent face action units) and heart rate seemed to be associated with the subjective ratings. The direction of correlation was not always equal across participants.

It is likely that the quality of the emotional ratings differs between participants. Some people cannot or will not report emotions very accurately, so we would expect that for them, no correlations will be found while for others it is possible. Indeed for some participants, only about 8% of the correlations were significant (i.e. around chance level) while for the best participant, almost 50% was. Leaving out correlations with face action units that seemed not informative in general, the highest score was even 70%.

Pairs of variables

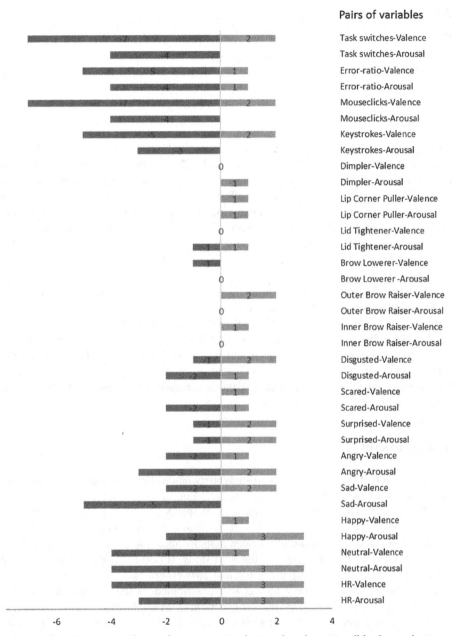

Number of participants with significant negative (orange) and positive (blue) correlations

Fig. 4. Number of participants (out of 16) with significant correlations between rated emotional state and unobtrusive measures as indicated on the right (from top to bottom measures reflecting computer activity, facial expression and heart rate). Numbers are indicated as negative for negative correlations and positive for positive correlations. (Color figure online)

3.3   Classification

Classification accuracy averaged across accuracies per participant was 59% for valence (with 7 out of 16 participants showing significantly above chance classification of 50%) and 58% (with 5 out of 16 participants showing significantly above chance classification) for arousal.

3.4   Interviews

Participants generally liked the experiment (on a scale from 1 to 10, M = 7.3, SD = 1.1) and would participate again (M = 7.5, SD = 1.2). They reported that the affect grid was easy and quick to use, though participants also stated that at times it was challenging to indicate their 'true' emotional state. The affect grid was not experienced as interfering or bothering, except in a few cases when participants were very concentrated and wanted to finish a task. The unobtrusive recordings (Mio wrist band, web cam and computer activity logging) were indeed experienced as unobtrusive. Most participants thought that the recordings did not make them behave differently, they reported that awareness of being monitored decreased over time.

Opinions differed on wanting to use a potential application that could arise from research like this: 'an application that can provide insight in personal stress levels and generate advice based on this' (M = 5.0, SD = 2.4). Disadvantages that were mentioned were privacy issues, a lack of trust that it would work and the feeling that they are already aware of their stress level and thus would not need such an application. Privacy issues arose with some (not all) imagined practical applications: 15 out of 16 participants said to be willing to share data on a personal level with a doctor, 8 with their manager, and 5 with colleagues.

4   Discussion

The approach that we followed here to study associations between implicit, unobtrusive measures on the one hand and self-reported emotion in a natural, real life situation on the other hand, led to a strong adherence of participants. Despite the obligation to come to the recording facilities for 10 days, to respond to a pop-up every 15 min, and a low financial reward, only three out of nineteen participants did not finish the study and one participated longer than required. In the total study, it occurred only a few times that participants clicked the pop-up away without answering. As confirmed by the participants in the interviews, likely factors that contributed to this success are that the recorded implicit variables were indeed experienced as unobtrusive, that the emotion was probed with only one click (which was easy and quick, and not too annoying). Furthermore, participants valued the working space and the pre-scheduled working time to be devoted to their personal projects. Participants signed up completely voluntarily to the study, knowing about the requirements and measurements.

In a real-life office environment we found associations between heart rate, global facial expression, and computer activity on the one hand and currently experienced valence and arousal on the other hand. The direction of the associations were not consistent across participants.

For heart rate, one may intuitively expect that heart rate increases with arousal. We did find a positive correlation for some individuals, but for others the correlation was negative. In fact, the literature shows that the relation between heart rate and arousal can go both ways. In our own studies, we found instances of positive relations, e.g. in social stress [20] and negative relations, e.g. when reading arousing sections in a novel [21]. The reason for this is probably that self-reported arousal can be associated with the body being prepared for action, cf. the defense reflex, or with a concentrated, focused state, cf. the orienting reflex where receptive and consolidating processes are facilitated [22]. With the defense system heart rate accelerations were found, while with the orienting system decelerations in heart rate were found [23].

. For overall face expression, consistent directions would have been expected since the emotions covary with a certain level of valence and arousal. For instance, since anger is an emotion with low valence and high arousal [24], one would expect significant correlations between reported valence to be negative, and correlations with arousal to be positive. Such consistent patterns are not shown (Fig. 4). It might have been hard for the facial expression recognition algorithm to correctly interpret facial expressions in the office context, because facial expressions have a strong communicative function and in the present context, participants were not communicating with other individuals. One might therefore attribute the observed, across-participants, lack of coherence between facial expressions and subjective states to the fact that the studied context did not (or hardly) involve social interaction in the study. Note that even though the higher level interpretation of action units as performed by the face expression algorithm did not correctly predict the type of subjective state, it still provided information about valence and arousal as indicated by the number of participants that showed significant correlations (Fig. 4).

For computer activity the varying directions of correlations between participants were not unexpected. Some individuals are happy when they type a lot and are productive, for others it may be an indication that they have time pressure and feel negatively stressed.

The subjective rating plots, the correlation- and classification results suggest that some of the essential requirements to be able to proceed in the attempt to monitor emotion during real life office work are met: emotions under real life office working circumstances seem to vary enough, and can be reported well enough, in order to uncover relations with several unobtrusively measured variables on the level of an individual person. This opens the way for monitoring in real life that is more fine-grained than the frequency with which emotion is probed, which would be useful for research and application purposes. However, associations and classifications as reported here are still very modest or nonexistent for part of the participants.

There are several ways in which correlations and classification can be improved. Data from different (shorter) time intervals than the currently used 15 min preceding reported current emotion for all variables may better reflect current emotion. Context could be further specified by considering data per application (type) or use application (type) as a feature, or by adding adaptive learning of contexts [25]. Unreliable data (especially computer interaction data) could be excluded by using a criterion on the percentage of the time that participants were actually at the computer during the used data interval. Future analyses should also focus on obtaining a deeper understanding of what is happening. When or for whom do we see which associations? Results of personality questionnaires or questionnaires on working habits and coping styles could be taken into account. Are the different tasks (applications) causing or hiding the associations? For instance, users will show a higher rate of key presses when using text processing applications than when using a web browser. When a user is more happy when browsing the web than using a text processing application, the application may be the underlying reason for key presses to be informative on mental state. On the other hand, while the number of keypresses may be informative about mental state in the word processing case, it may not be in the web browsing case; and the former association may be lost when data from all applications are taken together.

When sufficient classification accuracy can be reached, simulation of a real time situation would be of interest - training a model on successively incoming data and predict subsequent subjective rating. For future studies, it would be helpful and feasible to include eye tracker information (pupil size and blink features) as well as information about posture (which could also take the form of distance between the head and the webcam).

Acknowledgements. We would like to thank our TNO colleagues Bart Joosten and Thymen Wabeke for the technical setup; Leon Wiertz from Noldus for help with the face reader data; Jan-Willem Streefkerk (TNO) for project management. This publication was supported by the Dutch national program COMMIT (project P7 SWELL), and TNO Early Research Programs Making Sense of Big Data (Judith Dijk) and Human Enhancement.

References

1. Byrne, E.A., Parasuraman, R.: Psychophysiology and adaptive automation. Biol. Psychol. **42**(3), 249–268 (1996)
2. Baddeley, J.L., Pennebaker, J.W., Beevers, C.G.: Everyday social behavior during a major depressive episode. Soc. Psychol. Personal. Sci. **4**(4), 445–452 (2013)
3. Platt, T., Hofmann, J., Ruch, W., Proyer, R.T.: Duchenne display responses towards sixteen enjoyable emotions: individual differences between no and fear of being laughed at. Motiv. Emotion **37**(4), 776–786 (2013)
4. Koldijk, S., Sappelli, M., Verberne, S., Neerincx, M.A., Kraaij, W.: The SWELL knowledge work dataset for stress and user modeling research. In: Proceedings of the 16th ACM International Conference on Multimodal Interaction, pp. 291–298 (2014)
5. Koldijk, S., Neerincx, M.A., Kraaij, W.: Detecting work stress in offices by combining unobtrusive sensors. IEEE Trans. Affect. Comput. (2016)
6. Hogervorst, M.A., Brouwer, A.-M., van Erp, J.B.F.: Combining and comparing EEG, peripheral physiology and eye-related measures for the assessment of mental workload. Front. Neurosci. **8**, 322 (2014)
7. Okada, Y., Yoto, T.Y., Suzuki, T., Sakuragawa, S., Sugiura, T.: Wearable ECG recorder with acceleration sensors for monitoring daily stress: office work simulation study. In: Conference Proceedings: Annual International Conference of the IEEE Engineering in Medicine and Biology Society, IEEE Engineering in Medicine and Biology Society, Annual Conference, pp. 4718–4721 (2013)

8. Alberdi, A., Aztiria, A., Basarab, A.: Towards an automatic early stress recognition system for office environments based on multimodal measurements: a review. J. Biomed. Inform. **59**, 49–75 (2016)

9. Brouwer, A.-M., Zander, T.O., van Erp, J.B.F., Korteling, J.E., Bronkhorst, A.W.: Using neurophysiological signals that reflect cognitive or affective state: six recommendations to avoid common pitfalls. Front. Neurosci. **9**, 136 (2015)

10. van Os, J., Delespaul, P., Barge, D., Bakker, R.P.: Testing an mHealth momentary assessment routine outcome monitoring application: a focus on restoration of daily life positive mood states. PLoS ONE **9**(12), e115254 (2014)

11. Mark, G., Iqbal, S.T., Czerwinski, M., Johns, P.: Bored mondays and focused afternoons: the rhythm of attention and online activity in the workplace. In: Proceedings of the SIGCHI Conference on Human Factors in Computing Systems, pp. 3025–3034 (2014)

12. Trull, T.J., Ebner-Priemer, U.: Ambulatory assessment. Annu. Rev. Clin. Psychol. **9**, 151–176 (2013)

13. Moskowitz, D.S., Young, S.N.: Ecological momentary assessment: what it is and why it is a method of the future in clinical psychopharmacology. J. Psychiatry Neurosci. **31**(1), 13–20 (2006)

14. Kreibig, S.D.: Autonomic nervous system activity in emotion: a review. Biol. Psychol. **84**, 394–421 (2010)

15. Craig, S.D., D'Mello, S., Witherspoon, A., Graesser, A.: Emote aloud during learning with AutoTutor: applying the Facial Action Coding System to cognitive–affective states during learning. Cogn. Emot. **22**(5), 777–788 (2008)

16. Ekman, P., Friesen, W.V., Hager, J.: The Facial Action Coding System (FACS): A Technique for the Measurement of Facial Action. Consulting Psychologists Press, Inc., Palo Alto (1978)

17. Russel, J.A., Weiss, A., Mendelsohn, G.A.: Affect grid: a single-item scale of pleasure and arousal. J. Pers. Soc. Psychol. **57**(3), 493–502 (1989)

18. Van Gerven, M., Bahramisharif, A., Farquhar, J., Heskes, T.: Donders Machine Learning Toolbox (DMLT) for matlab from https://github.com/distrep/DMLT, version 26 June 2013 (2013)

19. Oostenveld, R., Fries, P., Maris, E., Schoffelen, J.M.: FieldTrip: open source software for advanced analysis of MEG, EEG, and invasive electrophysiological data. Comput. Intell. Neurosci. (2011). Article ID 156869

20. Brouwer, A.M., Hogervorst, M.A.: A new paradigm to induce mental stress: the Sing-a-Song Stress Test (SSST). Front. Neurosci. **8**, 224 (2014)

21. Brouwer, A.M., Hogervorst, M.A., Reuderink, B., van der Werf, Y., van Erp, J.B.F.: Physiological signals distinguish between reading emotional and non-emotional sections in a novel. Brain-Comput. Interfaces **2**(2–3), 76–89 (2015)

22. Sokolov, E.N.: Higher nervous functions: the orienting reflex. Annu. Rev. Physiol. **25**(1), 545–580 (1963)

23. Graham, F.K., Clifton, R.K.: Heart-rate change as a component of the orienting response. Psychol. Bull. **65**(5), 305 (1966)

24. Posner, J., Russell, J.A., Peterson, B.S.: The circumplex model of affect: an integrative approach to affective neuroscience, cognitive development, and psychopathology. Dev. Psychopathol. **17**(3), 715–734 (2005)

25. Sappelli, M., Verberne, S., Kraaij, W.: Adapting the interactive activation model for context recognition and identification. ACM Trans. Interact. Intell. Syst. **6**(3) (2016). Article 22

Alpha and Theta EEG Variations as Indices of Listening Effort to Be Implemented in Neurofeedback Among Cochlear Implant Users

Giulia Cartocci[1(✉)], Anton Giulio Maglione[1], Dario Rossi[1],
Enrica Modica[1], Gianluca Borghini[3], Paolo Malerba[2],
Lucia Oriella Piccioni[4], and Fabio Babiloni[1]

[1] Sapienza University, Rome, Italy
giulia.cartocci@uniromal.it
[2] Cochlear Italia srl, Bologna, Italy
[3] IRCCS Fondazione Santa Lucia, Rome, Italy
[4] San Raffaele Hospital, Milan, Italy

Abstract. Theta and Alpha EEG rhythms appear useful for the listening effort estimation. In particular, Alpha would inhibit irrelevant stimuli, and Theta underlies working memory and processing. The balance between them seems essential for the word recognition, therefore evaluating the listening effort experienced by hearing impaired patients appears worthy, since noise/distortions in a speech signal increase listening effort. Aim of the study was the estimation of the effort during word in noise recognition under different noise conditions, and along the task. Results showed an increase in the frontal Theta and parietal Alpha for a difficult (but not the most difficult) noise condition, and for Theta in correspondence of the stimulus. Additionally, frontal Theta activity increased along the task for the same difficult noise condition during and after the stimulus.

This evaluation was preliminary for a neurofeedback application of the effort management by CI users, since it could affect performances and attitudes. Such assessment appears extremely worthy of investigation since the symbiotic interaction between cochlear implant devices and deaf patients for the decoding and processing of the incoming auditory signal.

Keywords: Workload index · Auditory · Word in noise recognition

1 Introduction

The balance between excitatory and inhibitory influences, and the capability of its adaptation, in order for the system to cope with situational demands, is at the basis of normal cognitive functioning. Several evidences (for a review Weisz et al. 2011) support the hypothesis that Alpha rhythm (~ 8–12 Hz) mirrors this excitatory-inhibitory balance, being the dominant rhythm at rest and decreasing in power (desynchronization) in correspondence of the stimuli anticipation and processing (Thut et al. 2006). Evidences

© Springer International Publishing AG, part of Springer Nature 2018
J. Ham et al. (Eds.): Symbiotic 2017, LNCS 10727, pp. 30–41, 2018.
https://doi.org/10.1007/978-3-319-91593-7_4

from visual and somatosensory domains provide a well-established knowledge of the occurrence of these Alpha-related excitatory and inhibitory states, but also a role for Theta ($\sim$4–8 Hz) in the stimuli encoding (Klimesch 1999). However, the investigation of Alpha and Theta rhythms involvement in "handling" auditory stimuli is a recent issue.

The listening effort, defined as "the mental exertion required to attend to, and understand, an auditory message" (McGarrigle et al. 2014) is a matter receiving wide interest in the scientific community. Beyond self-report data, multiple evidences highlight a role of frontal Theta and posterior Alpha EEG rhythms variation for the estimation of the listening effort and the processing of the acoustic signal also under adverse conditions (e.g. irrelevant acoustic input) (Cartocci et al. 2015). In this context, Theta activity has been evidenced to reflect working memory and lexico-semantic processing for Theta (Strauß et al. 2014; Wisniewski et al. 2015). In addition, data from noise vocoded speech experiment, revealed Theta power increases in frontotemporal channels at the presentation of more acoustic details (Obleser and Weisz 2012), so in correspondence of more available auditory information to be processed.

On the other hand, increases in Alpha power reflect active suppression of the to-be-ignored stimulus stream. Alpha-band power has been shown to increase over cortical areas responsible for processing irrelevant/distracting stimuli. These increases in Alpha power have been showed to occur prior to the arrival of an anticipated stimulus, so shading an anticipatory/preparatory role of Alpha (Foxe and Snyder 2011). It has been evidenced that the extent of the Alpha activity suppression would influence the speech intelligibility (Obleser and Weisz 2012), probably in relation to less need for functional inhibition and less demanding speech processing (Klimesch et al. 2007; Jensen and Mazaheri 2010; Weisz et al. 2011).

Alpha power increased at central–parietal sensors as function of acoustic degradation (higher alpha power with more severe acoustic degradation) (Obleser et al. 2012; Petersen et al. 2015).

In this scenario where the balance between these two rhythms seems essential for the correct word recognition, the evaluation of the listening effort experienced by hearing impaired patients appears worthy, since the presence of noise or distortions in a speech signal increases cognitive demand and listening effort (Stenfelt & Rönnberg 2009). In fact hearing impaired participants experience increased effort and/or stress during speech recognition in noisy conditions in comparison to normal hearing (NH) listeners (Asp et al. 2015; Caldwell and Nittrouer, 2013; Wendt et al. 2016). Research concerning hearing disorders through EEG techniques has already been useful in identifying altered patterns in patients, for instance in tinnitus patients (Attanasio et al. 2013; Cartocci et al. 2012; Weisz et al. 2005). In this kind of patients, neurofeedback techniques have been employed, reporting successful modification of the EEG pattern and in parallel of the clinical symptoms (Weiler et al. 2002; Dohrmann et al. 2007). In addition, listening effort levels may change between CI processing conditions for which speech intelligibility remains constant (Pals et al. 2013), to this end the investigation of the EEG patterns in CI users seems fundamental for the management of the cognitive resources to face word detection and processing in adverse listening conditions. In fact, despite high behavioral performances, the underlying effort experienced could be higher under adverse listening conditions, such as not using a noise reduction filter in correspondence of speech in noise listening

(Cartocci et al. 2016). The identification of EEG patterns underlying the facing of challenging listening conditions, beyond behavioral performances, would imply a path for the application of neurofeedback approach to the cognitive resources management in these patients, resulting in an ameliorated auditory process functioning. Such assessment appears extremely worthy of investigation since the symbiotic interaction between cochlear implant devices and deaf patients for the decoding and processing of the incoming auditory signal.

The ratio between the frontal Theta and parietal Alpha power, the workload index (IWL) (Klimesch 1999), has been indicated as an index of cognitive load in different contexts such as in avionics on pilots and air traffic controllers (Aricò et al. 2014; Borghini et al. 2014, 2015; Di Flumeri et al. 2015). Indeed, such studies described the correlation of spectral power of the EEG with the complexity of the task that the user was performing. In fact, an increase of the frontal EEG power spectra in the theta band (4–7 Hz) and a simultaneous decrease in the parietal EEG power spectra in the alpha band (8–12 Hz) have been observed when the required mental workload increases. Finally, the IWL application has been already approached to hearing impaired participants in the comparison among sound processors and noise reduction filters use (Cartocci et al. 2016), but also among noise conditions (Cartocci et al. 2015), providing evidences of IWL discrimination capabilities among the various experimental conditions (see further in the text).

Therefore, aim of the present study was the assessment of the listening effort during a word in noise recognition under different background noise conditions, and along the execution of the task. This evaluation would be preliminary for a neurofeedback application of the effort management by such particular kind of participants, in whom the experienced cognitive effort could affect their performances

2 Methods

2.1 Participants and Protocol

The experimental sample was constituted by 9 adult CI users (mean age 51.22 ± 17.77), 3 of them presenting the CI in their left ear and 6 in the right ear. All participants were given of detailed information about the study and signed an informed consent. Participants were volunteers, who did not receive any compensation from taking part in the study. The experiment was performed in accord to the principles outlined in the Declaration of Helsinki of 1975, as revised in 2000, and it was approved by the Sapienza University of Rome ethical committee in charge for the Department of Molecular Medicine. Participants were sitting on a comfortable chair in front of a computer and instructed to limit unnecessary movements as much as possible. Participants performed a forced-choice word recognition task, in which stimuli consisted of Italian disyllabic words from "Audiometria Vocale GNResound" (Turrini et al. 1993), delivered free-field at an intensity of 65 dB HL. Loudspeakers were set 1 m from the patient. The background noise was babble noise continuously delivered by loudspeakers. During EEG recordings, the noise was kept constant at 55 dB HL (SNR = +10).

The experimental protocol was composed by four noise conditions:

- Quiet condition: the signal was delivered in absence of background noise from two loudspeakers placed +45° and −45° in relation to the patient
- Bilateral Noise condition: the noise was delivered from two loudspeakers placed +45° and −45° in relation to the patient
- Noise to the Better Ear condition: the noise was delivered to the hearing ear of the patient (+90° or −90° depending on the side of the deafness) while the signal was delivered frontally (0°)
- Noise to the Worse Ear condition: the noise was delivered to the deaf ear of the patient (+90° or −90° depending on the side of the deafness) while the signal was delivered frontally (0°)

Each noise condition comprised 20 trials, corresponding to 20 words randomly presented, each trial was constituted by 4 phases: Pre-Word, Word, Pre-Choice and Choice. The former three phases lasted 1 s, at the end of the Pre-Choice phase there was the Choice phase lasting maximum 5 s depending on the response time, resulting in a trial with a maximum 8 s length. The investigated phases were:

- Pre-Word: the phase preceding the listening of the target words
- Word: the phase corresponding to the listening of the target words
- Pre-Choice: the phase preceding the request of a response from the participant.

These three phases have been selected for the analysis in order to investigate the EEG activity preparatory to the stimulus delivery, the perception of the stimulus and the processing of it respectively. In correspondence of the Choice phase the participant was asked to choose and press one out of four colored buttons on a customized key-board, in order to select the just heard word stimulus among four words, that appeared each in a different colored box on the screen. The target word had the 25% of probability to appear in one of the four colored boxes and positions on the screen (top left, bottom left, top right, bottom right). This phase was excluded from the analysis because the focus of the present research was circumscribed to the only auditory phenomena occurring during the test, and not also in the reaction to the visual stimuli presented in the Choice phase. The noise conditions characterized by the presence of the background noise were randomly presented, while the Quiet condition has been always presented as first, and employed as baseline (see further in the Statistical Analysis section).

2.2 EEG Analysis

A digital ambulatory monitoring system (Bemicro EBNeuro, Italy) was used to record EEG. For the acquisition a 19 channels cap was used. Signals were acquired with a sampling frequency of 256 Hz end collected simultaneously during the experiment. A 50-Hz notch filter was applied to remove the power interference. A ground and a reference electrode were placed on the forehead and the impedances were maintained below 10 (kΩ). The EEG recording was filtered with a band pass filter (2–30 Hz) and then the Independent Component Analysis (ICA) was used to remove artifacts and blink component from the traces. In particular, for the ICA we used the *FastICA* algorithm (Marchini et al. 2013; Hyvarinen, 1999), and the averaged number of rejected components across the participants was of 2 components, one for the eyeblinks and the other for the eye gazes. Successively EEG recordings were segmented into trials.

Each trial was divided into Pre-Word, Word and Pre-Choice time segments. For each of these segments the Power Spectrum Density (PSD) was calculated, observing the EEG PSD values in Theta (4–8 Hz) and Alpha (8–12 Hz) bands. In particular, the *pwelch* algorithm implemented on Matlab has been used with the following parameters: Window: 2 s; Overlap: 0.125 s; Nfft = Window; Fs = 256 Hz (sample frequency). The Window-size has been chosen accordingly to the condition of stationarity of the EEG signal (Elul 1969). In fact, this is a necessary hypothesis in order to proceed with the spectral analysis of the EEG signal.

The workload index (IWL) was defined as the ratio between the EEG PSD in theta band over the central frontal area (F7, F8, F3, F4, Fz) and the EEG PSD in alpha band over the central parietal area (P7, P8, P3, P4, Pz) (Maglione et al. 2014).

2.3 Statistical Analysis

The Quiet condition has been used as baseline for the normalization of the experimental conditions presenting background noise. In order to normalize data, it has been performed the robust Z-score, as a function of median and median absolute deviation (MAD), defined as:

$$rz = |x - med(x)|/mad(x) \tag{1}$$

Where: rz stands for Robust Z-score; $med(x)$ stands for median of the Quiet condition; $mad(x)$ stands for MAD of the Quiet condition.

Repeated measure ANOVA has been performed on EEG data, considering the factor PHASE (with three levels: Pre-Word, Word and Pre-Choice) and the factor CONDITION (with three levels: Bilateral Noise, Noise to the Better Ear and Noise to the Worse Ear). Duncan post-hoc has been performed on significant effects and interactions. Simple regression has been performed in order to investigate the linear regression between the number of the trial and the corresponding Alpha, Theta or IWL values. The Bonferroni correction has been performed on the significant results obtained by the linear regression.

3 Results

3.1 Behavioral Results

The Quiet condition, with 10.83%, reported the lower percentage of errors in the word recognition task, while the noise condition that reported the higher percentage of errors, 53.33%, among participants was the Bilateral Noise (Fig. 1).

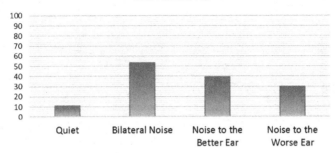

% of errors among the noise conditions

Fig. 1. Behavioral results reporting the percentage of errors obtained in each of the noise conditions in the word in noise recognition task.

3.2   Frontal Theta

It has been found a significant effect of the PHASE (F(2, 38) = 34.567 p < 0.001) (Fig. 2 left), with the Pre-Word phase obtaining the higher Theta values in comparison to the Word (p = 0.045) and the Pre-Choice phase (p < 0.001). The Pre-Choice phase was also lower than the Word phase (p < 0.001). In addition there was a significant effect of the CONDITION (F(2, 38) = 22.812 p < 0.001) (Fig. 2 center), characterized by higher values for the Noise to the Worse Ear condition in comparison to the Bilateral Noise and the Noise to the Better Ear conditions (p < 0.001 both), showing the last two conditions almost an overlapping pattern. Furthermore, there was a significant interaction PHASExCONDITION (F(4, 76) = 13.418 p < 0.001) (Fig. 2 right). Specifically, the Noise to the Worse Ear condition, reported higher values in the Pre-Word and Word phases (Pre-Word: Noise to the Worse Ear Vs Bilateral Noise p = 0.004; Pre-Word: Noise to the Worse Ear Vs Noise to the Better Ear p = 0.010; Word: Noise to the Worse Ear Vs Bilateral Noise p < 0.001; Word: Noise to the Worse Ear Vs Noise to the Better Ear p < 0.001), but not in the Pre-Choice phase (Pre-Choice phase: Noise to the Worse Ear Vs Bilateral Noise p = 0.708; Pre-Choice phase: Noise to the Worse Ear Vs Noise to the Better Ear p = 0.453). Additionally, the Noise to the Worse Ear condition in the Word phase showed the highest Theta values in comparison to all the other combinations of phases and conditions (p < 0.01 for all). Finally, the

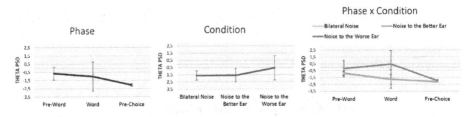

Fig. 2. Results for the Theta PSD analysis.

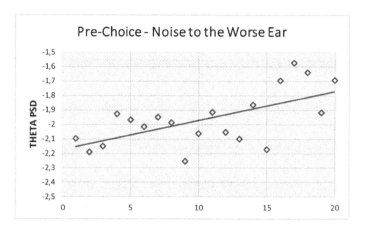

Fig. 3. Scatterplot representing the linear regression between Theta PSD values and the number of the trial for the Noise to the Worse Ear condition during the Pre-Choice phase.

simple regression analysis highlighted a correlation between the progressive number of the trial and the Theta values along the task for the Pre-Choice phase in the Noise to the Worse Ear condition (R = 0.629 p = 0.003) (Fig. 3).

3.3 Parietal Alpha

Alpha values analysis showed a significant effect of the PHASE (F(2,38) = 15.402 p < 0.001) (Fig. 4 left). Specifically, the Pre-Word phase reported higher values in comparison to the Word (p = 0.012) and Pre-Choice (p < 0.001) phases. In addition, the Pre-Choice phase obtained lower values in comparison to the Pre-Word (p < 0.001) and Word phase (p = 0.006). Also the effect of the CONDITION resulted statistically significant (F(2, 38) = 14.653 p < 0.001) (Fig. 4 center), characterized by higher values for the Noise to the Worse Ear condition in comparison to the Bilateral Noise and the Noise to the Better Ear conditions (both p < 0.001). Additionally, it was found a significant interaction PHASExCONDITION (F(4, 76) = 5.653 p < 0.001) (Fig. 4 right). In particular, the Noise to the Worse Ear condition in the Pre-Word phase reported the highest Alpha values in comparison to all the other conditions in all the phases (p < 0.001 for all).

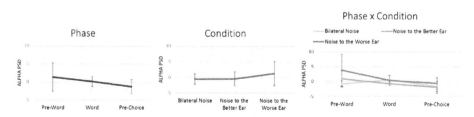

Fig. 4. Results for the Alpha PSD analysis.

3.4 Workload Index

It has been found a significant effect of the PHASE ($F(2, 38) = 74.943$ $p < 0.001$) (Fig. 5 left), characterized by a decrease in the Pre-Choice phase in comparison to the Pre-Word and Word phases ($p < 0.001$ both). Moreover, it was found a significant interaction PHASExCONDITION ($F(4, 76) = 15.063$ $p < 0.001$) (Fig. 5 right). In particular, the Noise to the Worse Ear condition in the Word phase showed the highest IWL levels ($p < 0.05$). In the same Word phase, it was possible to observe a statistical difference among all the noise condition, with the Bilateral Noise condition reporting the lower IWL values and the Noise to the Worse Ear condition the higher ones (Noise to the Worse Ear Vs Noise to the Better Ear $p = 0.001$; Noise to the Worse Ear Vs Bilateral Noise $p < 0.001$; Noise to the Better Ear Vs Bilateral Noise $p = 0.006$).

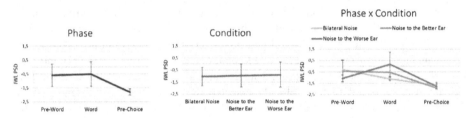

Fig. 5. Results for the IWL analysis.

4 Discussion

The evidence that the Noise to the Worse Ear condition, in which the participants heard the noise in the deaf ear and the signal frontally, reported the higher Theta values could be explained by the fact that this noise condition was difficult for the listener, but not impossible or, on the other hand, extremely easy. This consideration would imply high level of Theta, and so of listening effort and processing, in the Noise to the Worse Ear condition. Supporting this hypothesis there is the evidence reported by Wisniewski et al. (2017), who found an increase of frontal Theta activity in correspondence of difficult, but not easy nor impossible trials in a match to sample task. In this scenario, the Bilateral Noise and the Noise to the Better Ear conditions would have probably been perceived as overwhelming from a cerebral effort prospect. Previous studies concerning asymmetrical sensorineural hearing loss children showed an enhancement of Theta and IWL in the Noise to the Worse Ear condition (Cartocci et al. 2015), suggesting a different pattern of activity between children (usually pre-lingually deaf) and adults (usually post-lingually deaf), but also between different hearing amplification conditions. Concerning the first point, the difference between children and adults, it can be linked to the use of already existing speech sound networks in CI postlingually deafened patients (Naito et al. 2000), that could be lacking or different in children. Furthermore, evidences from the reaction to music, showed different patterns between children and adult CI users, as indexed by the Alpha frontal asymmetry (Cartocci et al. *in press*).

The correlation between the Theta values during the development of the task and the number of the trial, reported for the Noise to the Worse Ear condition in the Pre-Choice phase, suggests a progressive increase of the listening effort. This appears reasonable since the Pre-Choice phase presents, together with the Word phase, the major challenges of the task, that is the correct detection of the target word and the holding of the memory trace of the word for the further forced choice word recognition phase.

Alpha values, concerning the noise conditions, presented a pattern that could be explained by the evidence that parietal Alpha desynchronization reflects higher mental workload, whilst parietal Alpha synchronization lower mental workload (Klimesch 1999; Borghini et al. 2014). In fact, the Bilateral Noise and the Noise to the Better Ear condition would be more demanding so to elicit higher mental workload (Alpha desynchronization), while the Noise to the Worse Ear condition lower mental workload (Alpha synchronization).

The results about the strong decrease of both the Theta and Alpha activity during the Pre-Choice phase, characterized by the presence of the only background noise, before the appearance of the four colored boxes on the screen, could be linked to the disengagement from the attendance to the auditory stimulus (not expected) and also from the inhibition of the background noise since in this phase of the trial the participant was supposed to have already detected the target word, so listening effort would be minimum. Vice versa, considering the phase that reported higher values, that is the Pre-Word phase, the high Alpha values would reflect an inhibitory function toward irrelevant stimuli (Klimesch et al. 2007) in preparation of the stimulus reception, suggesting an anticipatory/preparatory role of Alpha (Foxe and Snyder 2011; Obleser and Weisz 2012). On the other hand, high Theta values in the preparatory phase would mirror a preparatory phase needed for the later memory encoding of the stimulus (Salari and Rose 2016).

The results concerning the IWL index in the Word phase, characterized by the simultaneous presence of the background noise and the target word, suggest a scale of listening effort for the detection of the stimulus, produced by the different noise conditions. Specifically, the Bilateral Noise condition elicited the lower IWL values and the Noise to the Worse Ear condition the higher. This latter evidence would be explained by the fact that the mixing of the signal and sound from the same sources could represent the most challenging situations, since the overlapping source of stimulus and noise was the most challenging for the patients to distinguish between these two kinds of sound and isolate the stimulus. Therefore, the Bilateral Noise condition would be so overdemanding to don't raise IWL levels (Cartocci et al. 2015). Supporting this hypothesis, behavioral results evidenced that the higher percentage of errors were reported in correspondence of the Bilateral Noise condition. The Noise to the Better Ear, on the other hand, would elicit high level of IWL, but in the context of an affordable task, so producing an IWL index increase.

Even if more investigation is needed, the sum of these evidences supports the capability of Alpha, Theta and IWL to detect auditory-related effort, in particular for the Theta power variation. The monitoring of these variations and the training for their control under adverse listening conditions would be extremely relevant for CI users, resulting in reduced effort levels and better management of their cognitive resources. Further studies employing statistics at a single participant level are needed toward the implementation of neurofeedback treatments for the management of challenging situations in hearing impaired patients, in order to design tailor-made interventions at the light of interindividual differences. Neurofeedback interventions have been already employed in hearing disorders patients, for example in tinnitus patients, where an increase in Alpha activity was associated to an amelioration of the symptoms and even the abolishment of the tinnitus sensation (Weiler et al. 2002; Dohrmann et al. 2007; Weisz et al. 2005; Weisz et al. 2011).

Acknowledgments. Giulia Cartocci and Anton Giulio Maglione equally contributed to the present paper.

References

Aricò, P., Borghini, G., Graziani, I., Taya, F., Sun, Y., Bezerianos, A., Thakor, N.V., Cincotti, F., Babiloni, F.: Towards a multimodal bioelectrical framework for the online mental workload evaluation. Presented at the 36th Annual International Conference of the IEEE Engineering in Medicine and Biology Society, New York (2014). https://doi.org/10.1109/embc.2014. 6944254

Asp, F., Mäki-Torkko, E., Karltorp, E., Harder, H., Hergils, L., Eskilsson, G., Stenfelt, S.: A longitudinal study of the bilateral benefit in children with bilateral cochlear implants. Int. J. Audiol. **54**(2), 77–88 (2015). https://doi.org/10.3109/14992027.2014.973536

Attanasio, G., Russo, F.Y., Roukos, R., Covelli, E., Cartocci, G., Saponara, M.: Sleep architecture variation in chronic tinnitus patients. Ear Hear. **34**(4), 503–507 (2013). https://doi.org/10.1097/AUD.0b013e31827bc436

Borghini, G., Aricò, P., Ferri, F., Graziani, I., Pozzi, S., Napoletano, L., Imbert, J.P., Granger, G., Benhacene, R., Babiloni, F.: A neurophysiological training evaluation metric for air traffic management. In: 2014 36th Annual International Conference of the IEEE Engineering in Medicine and Biology Society, pp. 3005–3008 (2014). https://doi.org/10.1109/embc.2014. 6944255

Borghini, G., Aricò, P., Flumeri, G.D., Salinari, S., Colosimo, A., Bonelli, S., Babiloni, F.: Avionic technology testing by using a cognitive neurometric index: a study with professional helicopter pilots. In: 2015 37th Annual International Conference of the IEEE Engineering in Medicine and Biology Society (EMBC), pp. 6182–6185 (2015). https://doi.org/10.1109/ EMBC.2015.7319804

Caldwell, A., Nittrouer, S.: Speech perception in noise by children with cochlear implants. J. Speech Lang. Hear. Res. JSLHR **56**(1), 13–30 (2013). https://doi.org/10.1044/1092-4388 (2012/11-0338

Cartocci, G., Maglione, A.G., Vecchiato, G., Modica, E., Rossi, D., Malerba, P., Marsella, P., Scorpecci, A., Giannantonio, S., Mosca, F., Leone, C.A., Grassia, R., Babiloni, F.: Frontal brain asymmetries as effective parameters to assess the quality of audiovisual stimuli perception in adult and young cochlear implant users. Acta Otorhinolaryngol. Ital. **37**, 1–15 (2017). https://doi.org/10.14639/0392-100X-1407

Cartocci, G., Maglione, A.G., Rossi, D., Modica, E., Malerba, P., Borghini, G., Di Flumeri, G., Aricò, P., Babiloni, F.: Applications in cochlear implants and avionic: examples of how neurometric measurements of the human perception could help the choice of appropriate human-machine interaction solutions beyond behavioral data. PsychNol. J. **14**(2–3), 117–133 (2016)

Cartocci, G., Maglione, A.G., Vecchiato, G., Di Flumeri, G., Colosimo, A., Scorpecci, A., Marsella, P., Giannantonio, S., Malerba, P., Borghini, G., Arico, P., Babiloni, F., Babiloni, F.: Mental workload estimations in unilateral deafened children. In: 2015 37th Annual International Conference of the IEEE Engineering in Medicine and Biology Society (EMBC), pp. 1654–1657 (2015). https://doi.org/10.1109/embc.2015.7318693

Cartocci, G., Attanasio, G., Fattapposta, F., Locuratolo, N., Mannarelli, D., Filipo, R.: An electrophysiological approach to tinnitus interpretation. Int. Tinnitus J. 17(2), 152–157 (2012). https://doi.org/10.5935/0946-5448.20120027

Di Flumeri, G., Borghini, G., Aricò, P., Colosimo, A., Pozzi, S., Bonelli, S., Golfetti, A., Kong, W., Babiloni, F.: On the use of cognitive neurometric indexes in aeronautic and air traffic management environments. In: Blankertz, B., Jacucci, G., Gamberini, L., Spagnolli, A., Freeman, J. (eds.) Symbiotic 2015. LNCS, vol. 9359, pp. 45–56. Springer, Cham (2015). https://doi.org/10.1007/978-3-319-24917-9_5

Dohrmann, K., Weisz, N., Schlee, W., Hartmann, T., Elbert, T.: Neurofeedback for treating tinnitus. In: Langguth, B., Hajak, G., Kleinjung, T., Cacace, A., Møller, A.R. (eds.) Progress in Brain Research, vol. 166, pp. 473–554. Elsevier, Amsterdam (2007). https://doi.org/10.1016/s0079-6123(07)66046-4

Elul, R.: Gaussian behavior of the electroencephalogram: changes during performance of mental task. Science 164, 328–331 (1969). https://doi.org/10.1126/science.164.3877.328

Foxe, J.J., Snyder, A.C.: The role of alpha-band brain oscillations as a sensory suppression mechanism during selective attention. Front. Psychol. 2, 154 (2011). https://doi.org/10.3389/fpsyg.2011.00154

Hyvarinen, A.: Fast and robust fixed-point algorithms for independent component analysis. IEEE Trans. Neural Netw. 10(3), 626–634 (1999)

Jensen, O., Mazaheri, A.: Shaping functional architecture by oscillatory alpha activity: gating by inhibition. Front. Hum. Neurosci. 4 (2010). https://doi.org/10.3389/fnhum.2010.00186

Klimesch, W.: EEG alpha and theta oscillations reflect cognitive and memory performance: a review and analysis. Brain Res. Rev. 29(2–3), 169–195 (1999). https://doi.org/10.1016/S0165-0173(98)00056-3

Klimesch, W., Sauseng, P., Hanslmayr, S.: EEG alpha oscillations: the inhibition–timing hypothesis. Brain Res. Rev. 53(1), 63–88 (2007). https://doi.org/10.1016/j.brainresrev.2006.06.003

Maglione, A., Borghini, G., Aricò, P., Borgia, F., Graziani, I., Colosimo, A., Kong, W., Vecchiato, G., Babiloni, F.: Evaluation of the workload and drowsiness during car driving by using high resolution EEG activity and neurophysiologic indices. In: Conference Proceedings: 2014 Annual International Conference of the IEEE Engineering in Medicine and Biology Society, pp. 6238–6241 (2014). https://doi.org/10.1109/embc.2014.6945054

Marchini, J.L., Heaton, C., Ripley, B.D.: fastICA: FastICA algorithms to perform ICA and Projection Pursuit. R package version, 1–2 (2013)

McGarrigle, R., Munro, K.J., Dawes, P., Stewart, A.J., Moore, D.R., Barry, J.G., Amitay, S.: Listening effort and fatigue: What exactly are we measuring? A British Society of Audiology Cognition in Hearing Special Interest Group 'white paper'. Int. J. Audiol. 53, 433–445 (2014). https://doi.org/10.3109/14992027.2014.890296

Naito, Y., Tateya, I., Fujiki, N., Hirano, S., Ishizu, K., Nagahama, Y., Fukuyama, H., Kojima, H.: Increased cortical activation during hearing of speech in cochlear implant users. Hear. Res. 143(1–2), 139–146 (2000)

Obleser, J., Weisz, N.: Suppressed alpha oscillations predict intelligibility of speech and its acoustic details. Cereb. Cortex (New York, NY) 22(11), 2466–2477 (2012). https://doi.org/10.1093/cercor/bhr325

Obleser, J., Wöstmann, M., Hellbernd, N., Wilsch, A., Maess, B.: Adverse listening conditions and memory load drive a common alpha oscillatory network. J. Neurosci. **32**(36), 12376–12383 (2012). https://doi.org/10.1523/JNEUROSCI.4908-11.2012

Pals, C., Sarampalis, A., Baskent, D.: Listening effort with cochlear implant simulations. J. Speech Lang. Hear. Res. JSLHR **56**(4), 1075–1084 (2013). https://doi.org/10.1044/1092-4388(2012/12-0074)

Petersen, E.B.: Wöstmann, M., Obleser, J., Stenfelt, S., Lunner, T.: Hearing loss impacts neural alpha oscillations under adverse listening conditions. Front. Psychol. **6**, 177 (2015). https://doi.org/10.3389/fpsyg.2015.00177

Salari, N., Rose, M.: Dissociation of the functional relevance of different pre-stimulus oscillatory activity for memory formation. Neuroimage **125**, 1013–1021 (2016). https://doi.org/10.1016/j.neuroimage.2015.10.037

Stenfelt, S., Rönnberg, J.: The signal-cognition interface: interactions between degraded auditory signals and cognitive processes. Scand. J. Psychol. **50**, 385–393 (2009). https://doi.org/10.1111/j.1467-9450.2009.00748.x

Strauß, A., Kotz, S.A., Scharinger, M., Obleser, J.: Alpha and theta brain oscillations index dissociable processes in spoken word recognition. Neuroimage **97**, 387–395 (2014). https://doi.org/10.1016/j.neuroimage.2014.04.005

Thut, G., Nietzel, A., Brandt, S.A., Pascual-Leone, A.: Alpha-band electroencephalographic activity over occipital cortex indexes visuospatial attention bias and predicts visual target detection. J. Neurosci. **26**, 9494–9502 (2006). https://doi.org/10.1523/JNEUROSCI.0875-06.2006

Turrini, M., Cutugno, F., Maturi, P., Prosser, S., Leoni, F.A., Arslan, E.: Bisyllabic words for speech audiometry: a new italian material. Acta Otorhinolaryngol. Ital. Organo Ufficiale Della Società Italiana Di Otorinolaringologia E Chirurgia Cervico-Facciale **13**(1), 63–77 (1993)

Weiler, E.W., Brill, K., Tachiki, K.H., Schneider, D.: Neurofeedback and quantitative electroencephalography. Int. Tinnitus J. **8**(2), 87–93 (2002)

Weisz, N., Hartmann, T., Müller, N., Lorenz, I., Obleser, J.: Alpha rhythms in audition: cognitive and clinical perspectives. Front. Psychol. **2**, 73 (2011). https://doi.org/10.3389/fpsyg.2011.00073

Weisz, N., Moratti, S., Meinzer, M., Dohrmann, K., Elbert, T.: Tinnitus perception and distress is related to abnormal spontaneous brain activity as measured by magnetoencephalography. PLoS Med. **2**(6), e153 (2005). https://doi.org/10.1371/journal.pmed.0020153

Wisniewski, M.G., Thompson, E.R., Iyer, N., Estepp, J.R., Goder-Reiser, M.N., Sullivan, S.C.: Frontal midline θ power as an index of listening effort. Neuroreport **26**, 94–99 (2015). https://doi.org/10.1097/WNR.0000000000000306

Wisniewski, M.G., Thompson, E.R., Iyer, N.: Theta- and alpha-power enhancements in the electroencephalogram as an auditory delayed match-to-sample task becomes impossibly difficult. Psychophysiology **54**, 1916–1928 (2017). https://doi.org/10.1111/psyp.12968

Wendt, D., Dau, T., Hjortkjær, J.: Impact of background noise and sentence complexity on processing demands during sentence comprehension. Front. Psychol. **7** (2016). https://doi.org/10.3389/fpsyg.2016.00345

Contextual Consistency as an Improvement to User Experience and System Transparency: The Case of a Vibrotactile Relaxation Device with Implicit Triggers

Luciano Gamberini[1], Francesca Freuli[1], Marta Nedves[1],
Walter Jensen[2], Ann Morrison[2], Valeria Orso[1], Giovanni Degiuli[1],
and Anna Spagnolli[1(✉)]

[1] University of Padua, Padua, Italy
{luciano.gamberini,anna.spagnolli}@unipd.it
[2] Aalborg University, Aalborg, Denmark

Abstract. In mobile devices for travellers and tourists, haptic stimulation is mainly employed to provide directions and alerts; but it could also be employed to influence the user's affective experience. Here we consider providing relaxing stimulation via a symbiotic vibrotactile vest and compare implicit triggers that are or not contextually consistent. We meet participants in the city center and walk them to a Point of Interest. During the walk, the vibrotactile vest provides them with relaxing stimulation either during waits (consistent condition) or while they walk (inconsistent condition). Participants, who are unaware of the trigger rationale, found the contextually consistent stimulation more pleasant, tended to consider it more transparent and useful. The results suggest that contextualized implicit triggers not only improve the user experience, but could also represent an intuitive strategy to increase the transparency of symbiotic systems.

Keywords: Vibrotactile wearable · Implicit data · Tourists · Transparency

1 Introduction

When finding their way towards an unusual destination or planning a new path according to changed travel conditions, current tourists and travelers can rely on mobile apps and devices to assist them [14]. The travelling experience, however, is not limited to successfully moving around to reach a Point of Interest (PoI): it is characterized by a richer set of emotions, affecting the intention to return to a destination or to recommend it to other people [18, 19]. Some of these emotions are positive, and some are not: traveling includes events that need to be born more than they are enjoyed, such as waiting in line or standing on crowded buses [4, 13]; travelers try to endure these events by using earphones, games and books [7, 10]. For this reason, within a larger project devoted to augmenting the tourist experience (CultAR project), we considered the use of a relaxing wearable, one that provides relaxing stimulation to relieve tourists/travelers during unpleasant moments of their visit.

© Springer International Publishing AG, part of Springer Nature 2018
J. Ham et al. (Eds.): Symbiotic 2017, LNCS 10727, pp. 42–52, 2018.
https://doi.org/10.1007/978-3-319-91593-7_5

The modality through which relaxing stimuli were conveyed was set to be vibrotactile. Vibrotactile stimulation is frequently used in mobile devices to notify the user of the proximity of a P.o.I. [20] or of a directional mistake [17]. They are considered advantageous compared with sound or visual notifications in that they do not require the user to interrupt their visual inspection of the surroundings or their conversation with the travel partners [16, 20]. Having those signals provided by a wearable would be even more convenient as the tourist would not need to carry any additional device in their hands. Based on these considerations, the relaxing device was designed as a vibrotactile vest, which is described more in detail in Sect. 2 below.

To assess the user experience with the vest, we imagined a scenario where the stimulation was automatically activated by some *symbiotic implicit trigger,* namely by a trigger autonomously detecting some predefined conditions in the users' behavior/state and starting the stimulation [6]. In our case, the symbiotic trigger was simulated with the so-called Wizard of Oz technique [5]. Such procedure is common when testing interfaces at a mockup or concept stage, and consists of creating the appearance of a working system for the user while in fact it is one of the experimenters (the wizard) who makes the system respond to the user ([10] p. 294). In this case, the participant wearing the vest was told that the device monitored the users' progress on a route and activated the relaxing stimulation autonomously, while in fact it was the researcher accompanying the participant who activated the stimulation under predefined circumstances.

The goal of the study was to test the response to the symbiotic trigger. More specifically, we checked whether the user responded differently to the stimulation when it was provided at moments consistent with its purpose even though s/he was unaware of how exactly the system made the decision. We preliminarily carried out some studies to identify which one of eight stimulation patterns available in the vest prototype that was mostly perceived as relaxing by users, and which part of a visit is usually considered as negative by tourists. Based on this, in the main study we activated the relaxing stimulation during the negative part of the visit, thereby producing a contextually consistent stimulation, or during the other parts of the visit, thereby producing a contextually inconsistent stimulation. Various dimensions of the users' experience were measured through a questionnaire.

The rest of the paper describes the vibrotactile vest used in the study; the two preliminary studies through which we defined which vibrotactile pattern was to be used and which events were to be included in the simulated visit; and the main study. The results are discussed in the final sections, also in terms of their implications for symbiotic systems' transparency.

2   The Vibrotactile Vest

The vibrotactile stimulations used in this study were administered by an actuator system sewn onto a commercially made summer sports vest where the fabric was breathable, stretchable, non-thermal and wicking. The stimulation was controlled by an application running on a tablet computer (Nvidia Shield Tablet running Android 5.1.1) and connected via Bluetooth to the vest. The tactile vest (Fig. 1) can deliver a total of eight affective stimulations. A team at Aalborg University designed the system. The 29 actuators were placed on the vest in a system that echoed an understanding of the body as a set of rhizome-like structures acting as communication tracks between the larger organs, practiced by many traditional medicines including Kinesiology, which works with principles of Traditional Chinese Medicine and modern muscle monitoring techniques [12, 15]. The developing team worked on the positioning and necessary combinations of actuators and patterns onto responsive points and zones of the body with an experienced kinesiologist trained in Neurophysiology. Kinesiology works with touch in a way that can be calming but may also be probing or jabbing running in sequences of jiggle, pause, jiggle (similar to saltation effect [8]) but largely running in longer duration, working on one area at a time and with longer pauses before moving to another area-system in order that the body processes and recovers from the prompts.

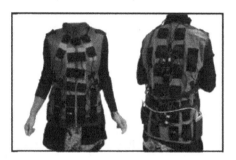

Fig. 1. The front and the back of vibrotactile vest with the actuators on it.

3   Preliminary Studies

3.1   Identifying a Relaxing Stimulation Pattern

A preliminary study aimed at identifying which of eight affective vibration patterns implemented in the vest was considered as relaxing by users. The study took place in a laboratory room. The session started with the participant being explained the goal of the study, signing the informed consent and receiving task instructions. S/he was then shown the vibrotactile vest and invited to wear it. Once ready, the experimenter administered the first stimulation by a Bluetooth-connected Android application running on a tablet. The participant was then asked to label the stimulation as either "relaxing" or "activating" (or to reply "I don't know") in the shortest possible time and the answer was entered in an electronic spreadsheet. Then the next stimulation was provided. After two sets of eight stimulations were completed, the participant was allowed to take a break. When s/he was ready to start again, the experimenter administered two more sets. This procedure was repeated until six different sets of the eight, randomly combined vibration patterns were administered.

A total of 14 participants volunteered for the experiment. Two participants were excluded from the analysis because they answered "I don't know" more than 40% of the times. Data analysis was thus conducted on a sample of 12 participants (6 women, 29.33 y.o. on average, $SD = 7.24$). Each stimulus was categorized 72 times in the sample. The percentage with which each stimulus was categorized as activating, relaxing or uncertain is shown in Fig. 2. The pattern that most frequently was assessed as relaxing was the one called 'Down'. However, a Mann-Whitney test revealed that such pattern was differently categorized by men and women, $U = 5$ $p = .032$: men judged it as relaxing in the 88.8% of the cases ($SD = 8.6$; $Mdn = 83.33$) while women did so in the 57.22% of the cases ($SD = 39.88$; $Mdn = 73.33$). Thus we selected the next best relaxing pattern, called 'Up'.

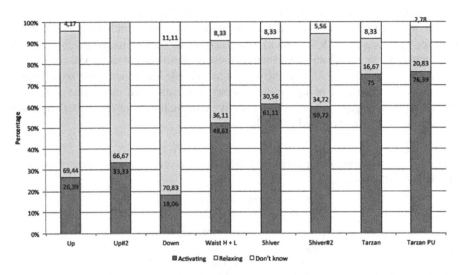

Fig. 2. Percentage of times the eight patterns were categorized by participants as activating, relaxing or uncertain.

The **Up** pattern thereby selected gives a smooth rolling up the spine effect (Fig. 3). It runs through 16 actuators that are evenly placed on either side upon the muscular ridge of the spine (eight each side). The pattern runs directionally from the base of the spine to the top of the neck with each paired set activated at the same time/interval. The Up pattern has an overall duration of 1400 ms. The ratio difference between overlap and duration is 1:2. The overlaps between the different actuators are designed to be smoothly following on, from one set of actuators to the next, thus there is no clear delineation of where one set of actuators stops vibrating and the next set begins, as if a hand stroked the spine.

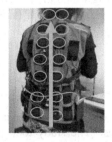

Fig. 3. Actuators active during the UP pattern of vibrations

3.2 Negative Moments in a Visit

In order to choose which events are generally considered as negative in a tourist visit or during a travel, we checked the literature on travel experience. Here queues, crowd and idleness are mentioned as typically negative events [4, 13]. To further corroborate our choice, we carried out a set of interviews to visitors met in the city center of two tourist cities, Padua and Bologna in Italy. After introducing the goal of the study, the interviewer asked on what occasions during the visit they used to feel bored, tired, unmotivated or stressed and on what occasion they felt instead in high spirits, excited, and happy. 70 people (42.9% women) were interviewed varying in age (44.34 years old on average, SD = 18.97) and provenance; most of them carried out a visit of the city for cultural purposes (80%). The answers were recorded and then analyzed independently by two members of the research team to identify and categorize the events bearing either a negative or a positive affective connotation. The researchers then met and agreed on the list reported in Table 1.

Table 1. Typical events during a visit and their affective connotation and percentage of the interviewees mentioning it.

Affective event	Affective connotation	
	Positive	Negative
Start	88%	12%
POI reached	92.9%	7.1%
I got lost	43.9%	34.1%
In line	11.7%	41.2%
Too crowded	–	88.9%
Meals	81.8%	9.1%
Poor directions	9.3%	91.7%
Fatigue	–	100%
Unexpected	78.9%	21.1%

Fatigue, poor directions, crowd, and queues emerged as main negative events from our interviews, confirming the suggestions already obtained from the literature. Among these, the most suitable negative event to implement in the procedure of our main study was 'waits', namely moments during which the participant was forced to stop walking to the destination by circumstances that were not under his/her control.

4 Main Study

4.1 Goal and Hypotheses

The main study investigates the user experience of the relaxing vibrotactile stimulation administered by the prototype vest. The study took place in the historical center of Padua in Italy, which was the site adopted by the CultAR project to test all prototypes;

in this study, participants walked to a historical building in the city to simulate a tourist visit. The historical building ('Loggia dei Carraresi'), although remarkable, was not a major tourist landmark and therefore it was more likely to be new and attractive to them. While walking they wore the vibrotactile vest; the route started near the clock tower in a city square and measured 180 m. In two predefined points along the itinerary, the participant was forced to stop (Fig. 4), the first time because the experimenter answered a phone call, and the second time because the experimenter was informed that a previous participant had yet to complete his/her tour.

Fig. 4. The route walked by the participants in the study with the two 'pause' icons to mark the points at which the participants were forced to stop. 'C' and 'I' letters mark the points at which the vibrotactile stimulation was administered respectively in the consistent and inconsistent condition (elaborated from GoogleMaps®).

The relaxing stimulation provided by the vest consisted of a set of three subsequent 'Up' vibrations lasting together about 5.6 s, thrice as long as in the preliminary experiment described in Sect. 3.1, to make it very clear and perceivable to the user. The vibrations were provided either during the waits (consistent condition) or while the participant was walking to the PoI (inconsistent condition). The conditions varied between participants. The rationale was that when the relaxing stimulation was provided during waits, it fitted the context in which it was administered since the participant was experiencing a typically negative event. In addition, during waits the participant had no other things to do: relaxing stimulations filled his/her time and were given fuller attention than while walking. For all these reasons, waits were more likely to be the right time for a relaxing vibration. Instead, the short, purposeful walk participants were engaged in during the rest of the session was comparatively more pleasant: it was not mentioned as a negative aspect neither by the literature nor in our interviews and represented also the very essence of the activity the participants volunteered to perform for us.

We expected the relaxing vibration to be received positively in both conditions, based on our preliminary study (H1), but more so in the consistent condition (H2).

4.2 Procedure

Tourists were approached in the city center. They were explained that we were testing the user experience of a vibrotactile vest designed to relax visitors during a tour. If they accepted to participate in the study they were asked to read the informed consent and to provide some background information (age and sex). Then the participant wore the vest and was provided one sample of the vibration. The experimenter explained that an application would activate the stimuli on the basis of the participants' position in the route to the destination; the exact criterion to trigger the stimulation was not disclosed to the user. As this study used a Wizard-of-Oz method, the stimulation was actually triggered by the experimenter through an Android tablet connected to the vest via Bluetooth. The participant was then shown a preview of the itinerary on Google Maps and was given information about the PoI, via photos and a brief oral recount in order to increase the interest in the tour [1]. Then the tour started. Once the PoI was reached, the post-session questionnaire was administered. To comply with ethics standards in research, at the end of the session the participant was explained that we adopted a Wizard-of-Oz procedure during the study and that the symbiotic mechanism was only simulated.

4.3 Measures

The users' post-session evaluations were collected with a questionnaire; the items, which were created ad hoc, are listed in the Appendix. We measured the perceived pleasantness (Items 1–5), opportunity (Items 6–9), fun (Items 10, 12, 13) and utility of the vibrations (Items 11, 14, 15, 16). We also evaluated the extent to which the system was perceived as responsive (Items 17–21), transparent (Items 22–23) and empathic (Items 24–26). The agreement with each statement was measured on a Likert scale ranging from 1 (I completely disagree) to 6 (I completely agree); the last 10 items also included an "I do not know" option. Participants' prior familiarity with the PoI was also asked.

4.4 Participants

In total 24 participants (19 women and 5 men) took part in the experiment, equally divided in the two conditions. The mean age of the sample was 24.58 (SD = 2.76). The participants were recruited on the road or via social networks and assigned to the two experimental conditions randomly at the start of the session. The data collected after the participant reached the destination confirmed that no participant was actually familiar with the PoI, which contributed to the realism of the simulated tourist visit.

4.5 Results

First we wanted to measure the participants' evaluation of the system, to see whether it was generally positive or not. We compared the questionnaire scores with the central value of the response scale (3.5) that was assumed to represent a neutral evaluation; we performed the comparison in each condition with two separate One Sample Wilcoxon Signed Rank Tests. The results show that participants evaluated the vibrations as pleasant, fun and suitable in both conditions (*p-values* ranged between 0.004 and 0.028). Regarding utility, it was significantly different from the central value of the response scale only in the consistent condition (*M = 4.58 Mdn* = 4.625 p = 0.004) (Fig. 5).

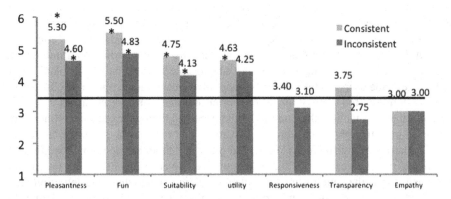

Fig. 5. Difference from middle point of the scale. Median scores for each evaluation dimension in the two conditions are displayed, with asterisks signaling a significant difference from the central value of the response scale (3.5).

We then tested whether the evaluations differed as an effect of the manipulation. A Mann-Whitney test was conducted on the mean ranks to compare the two conditions. The p-values were adjusted for multiple comparisons utilizing the Benjamini-Hochberg (BH) correction (Table 2). The test revealed a difference between the two conditions in the perceived pleasantness of the vibrations (z = −2.793, U = 24, p = 0.020 rg = 0.666), which was higher in the consistent condition (Table 2). Without the BH correction, fun and transparency were also significantly higher in the consistent condition.

Table 2. Results of inferential tests comparing questionnaires scores by condition (consistent vs. inconsistent).

	Pleasantness	Suitability	Fun	Utility	Responsiveness	Transparency	Empathy
Mann-Whitney U	24.000	47.000	34.500	45.000	49.500	37.500	64.000
Z	−2.793	−1.452	−2.200	−1.569	−1.304	−2.010	−.466
Exact. Sig.	.005	.1600	.028	.128	.198	.045	.671
Sig. (BH corr.)	0.020	0.160	0.056	0.160	0.297	0.135	0.671
Mean ranks (consistent)	16.500	14.580	15.62	14.750	14.380	15.380	13.17
Mean ranks (inconsistent)	8.500	10.420	9.38	10.250	10.620	9.620	11.83

5 Discussion and Conclusions

The results of the main study show that participants perceived the relaxing vibrations differently according to the condition. Although the relaxing stimulation was received positively in both conditions, confirming H1, the affective response in certain dimensions of the use experience was even more positive when the triggering circumstances were consistent with the purpose of the vibrations. In particular, the difference was significantly higher in the pleasantness scores; other constructs, although less sharply, seemed also to have been affected, in particular transparency and utility, pointing at the fact that somehow the users perceived the contextually consistent stimulations as more to the point. Surprisingly, users did not perceive the vest as more 'responsive' or 'empathic' when the trigger was contextually consistent; this was probably due to an infelicitous phrasing of the items referring to the system's being able to detect the users' 'plan', while a reference to the users' (physical) 'state' would have been more appropriate. Therefore H2 was confirmed for some of the user experience dimensions investigated.

To further substantiate the findings of the papers, additional experiments should be conducted investigating other vibrotactile patterns and unpleasant events during tourist visits. In particular, much work is needed in order to define the triggering condition for an actual symbiotic vest: in our study we simulated a very elementary one, based on a prolonged stop in the path toward a destination; but in a real system this definition must be refined (e.g. to exclude some stops that might not need relaxation, to define the threshold of movements that do not count as progress towards a destination, etc.) and personalized. Furthermore, we imagined basing our trigger on geolocal data, since it seemed relevant to a tourist visit and easily collectable via devices that are part of the regular equipment of any traveller (e.g., smart phones or tablets); but alternatively to geolocal data, or in combination with it, physiological or behavioural data could be used to detect the user's distress or fatigue (e.g., [2]). Also, while the sample size of the main study was enough to carry out inferential tests and to test the hypotheses, no generalization can be made on the overall appreciation of vibrotactile feedback by all types of visitors and under any visiting circumstances.

Regardless of the limits of this study, however, its findings are of broader interest than the specific case from which they have been obtained: first, they seem to suggest that contextually consistent triggers are worth being included in a device, as they might intensify its effect. Second, the fact that in the consistent condition the participants found the stimulations as more decidedly useful and the system as more transparent, suggests that the contextual consistency of an implicit trigger can play a role in increasing the transparency of symbiotic systems. While transparency is usually considered as the provision of explicit information about the criteria that generate a given result in a system [9], this study points at the possibility that intelligibility of a system derives from a good contextualization of the system output in the users' current activity without the need to explicitly expose the complex decisional tree followed by the system. Users might not grasp exactly the criteria used by the stem, but still perceive that the system makes sense and is consistent with their expectations. We think that this sort of 'tacit transparency' is worth being studied as the exploitation of implicit data and the deployment of Artificial Intelligence to automatize decisions becomes widespread [2].

Acknowledgments. The present work was partially funded by European Union Seventh Framework Program (FP7/2007–2013) under grant agreement No. 601139 (CultAR).

Appendix. Post-session Questionnaire

1	Overall, the vibrations I perceived during the tour were pleasant. (P)
2	The vibrations I perceived during the tour were similar to a massage. (P)
3	I believe that the vibrations relaxed me. (P)
4	The noise of the vibrations annoyed me. (P)
5	I believe that the vibrations were too long. (P)
6	Overall, the vibrations seemed suitable to me. (S)
7	I believe that the vibrations fitted the situation I was experiencing. (S)
8	I believe that the vibrations were given at the right moment of the tour. (S)
9	I believe that the vibrations were too intimate. (S)
10	Overall, the vibrations were fun. (F)
11	The vibrations increased the value of the visit. (U)
12	The vibrations tickled me. (F)
13	In the end I got tired of the vibrations. (F)
14	I believe that the device can improve the tourist experiences. (U)
15	I believe that relaxing during a tourist visit is useful. (U)
16	I believe it convenient that the device can automatically choose when to trigger the vibrations. (U)
I felt that the system…	
17	… was taking into account my previous actions on it. (R)
18	… responded like it knew what I wanted. (R)
19	… was responding to more than my explicit requests. (R)
20	… responded meaningfully. (R)
21	… anticipated what I was going to do next. (R)
22	… was an extension of my body. (T)
23	… was an extension of my brain. (T)
24	… was sensitive to my feelings. (E)
25	… helped me to refine my goals and objectives. (E)
26	… and I understood each other. (E)

P = pleasantness; S = suitability; F = fun; U = utility; R = responsiveness; T = transparency of the system; E = empathy

References

1. Bigne, J.E., Sanchez, M.I., Sanchez, J.: Tourism image, evaluation variables and after purchase behaviour: inter-relationship. Tour. Manag. **22**(6), 607–616 (2001)
2. Wilson, G.F., Russell, C.A.: Real-time assessment of mental workload using psychophysiological measures and artificial neural networks. Hum. Factors **45**(4), 635–644 (2003)

3. Cao, L.: Data science: a comprehensive overview. ACM Comput. Surv. (CSUR) **50**(3), 43 (2017)

4. Dawers, J., Rowley, J.: The waiting experience: towards service quality in the leisure industry. Int. J. Contemp. Hospitality Manage. **8**(1), 16–21 (1996)

5. Fraser, N.M., Gilbert, G.N.: Simulating speech systems. Comput. Speech Lang. **5**(1), 81–99 (1991)

6. Gamberini, L., Spagnolli, A.: Towards a definition of symbiotic relations between humans and machines. In: Gamberini, L., Spagnolli, A., Jacucci, G., Blankertz, B., Freeman, J. (eds.) Symbiotic 2016. LNCS, vol. 9961, pp. 1–4. Springer, Cham (2017). https://doi.org/10.1007/978-3-319-57753-1_1

7. Gamberini, L., Spagnolli, A., Miotto, A., Ferrari, E., Corradi, N., Furlan, S.: Passengers' activities during short trips on the London underground. Transportation **40**(2), 251–268 (2013)

8. Geldard, F.A.: Sensory Saltation: Metastability in the Perceptual World. Lawrence Erlbaum, Hillsdale (1975)

9. IEEE: The IEEE Global Initiative for Ethical Considerations in Artificial Intelligence and Autonomous Systems. Ethically Aligned Design: A Vision For Prioritizing Wellbeing With Artificial Intelligence And Autonomous Systems, Version 1 (2016). http://standards.ieee.org/develop/indconn/ec/autonomous_systems.html

10. Lazar, J., Feng, J.H., Hochheiser, H.: Research Methods in Human-Computer Interaction. Morgan Kaufmann, San Francisco (2017)

11. Lyons, G., Urry, J.: Travel time use in the information age. Transp. Res. Part A Policy Pract. **39**(2), 257–276 (2005)

12. Morrison, A., Knoche, H., Manresa-Yee, C.: Designing a vibrotactile language for a wearable vest. In: Marcus, A. (ed.) DUXU 2015. LNCS, vol. 9187, pp. 655–666. Springer, Cham (2015). https://doi.org/10.1007/978-3-319-20898-5_62

13. Nawijn, J.: Determinants of daily happiness on vacation. J. Travel Res. **50**(5), 559–566 (2011)

14. Neuhofer, B., Buhalis, D., Ladkin, A.: A typology of technology-enhanced tourism experiences. Int. J. Tourism Res. **16**(4), 340–350 (2014)

15. Neumann, D.A.: Kinesiology of the Musculoskeletal System: Foundations for Rehabilitation. Elsevier Health Sciences, St. Louis (2013)

16. Paneels, S., Roberts, J.C.: Review of designs for haptic data visualization. IEEE Trans. Haptics **3**(2), 119–137 (2010)

17. Pielot, M., Poppinga, B., Heuten, W., Boll, S.: PocketNavigator: studying tactile navigation systems in-situ. In: Proceedings of the SIGCHI Conference on Human Factors in Computing Systems, pp. 3131–3140. ACM, New York (2012)

18. Prayag, G., Hosany, S., Odeh, K.: The role of tourists' emotional experiences and satisfaction in understanding behavioral intentions. J. Destination Mark. Manage. **2**(2), 118–127 (2013)

19. Prayag, G., Hosany, S., Muskat, B., Del Chiappa, G.: Understanding the relationships between tourists' emotional experiences, perceived overall image, satisfaction, and intention to recommend. J. Travel Res. **56**(1), 41–54 (2015). https://doi.org/10.1177/0047287515620567

20. Szymczak, D., Rassmus-Gröhn, K., Magnusson, C., Hedvall, P.O.: A real-world study of an audio-tactile tourist guide. In: Proceedings of the 14th International Conference on Human-Computer Interaction with Mobile Devices and Services, pp. 335–344. ACM Press, New York (2012)

Effects of Monitor Refresh Rates
on c-VEP BCIs

Felix Gembler, Piotr Stawicki, Aya Rezeika, Abdul Saboor, Mihaly Benda,
and Ivan Volosyak$^{(\boxtimes)}$

Faculty of Technology and Bionics,
Rhine-Waal University of Applied Sciences, Kleve, Germany
ivan.volosyak@hochschule-rhein-waal.de
http://www.hochschule-rhein-waal.de

Abstract. Brain-Computer Interfaces (BCIs) allow humans to form a
physical symbiosis with computer systems. One use case scenario of
BCIs is communication by brain activity. High spelling speeds have been
achieved with BCIs based on code-modulated visual evoked potentials
(c-VEPs). Typically, the flickering stimuli are presented on a standard
60 Hz monitor. Users can find VEP-based BCIs annoying and tiring due
to the perceptible flickering. This is especially the case for multi-target
systems designed for maximal communication speed. Higher monitor
refresh rates allow a faster flickering rate for BCI targets, and thus a
more subtle visual stimulation. In this paper, user friendliness and speed
of c-VEP BCIs with different monitor refresh rates (60, 120 and 200 Hz)
are compared. The experiment was comprised of three sessions (each
consisting of training and spelling stages), one for each tested monitor
refresh rate. Performance was assessed with ITR and accuracy and user
friendliness was evaluated using a questionnaire. High flickering speed
is usually accompanied by poorer BCI performance. In this study, the
system utilizing the 200 Hz refresh rate surprisingly competed well in
terms of ITR and accuracy. Regarding user friendliness it was preferred
by most users, as expected.

Keywords: Brain-Computer Interface (BCI) · c-VEP · Refresh rate

1 Introduction

Brain-Computer Interfaces (BCIs) can provide communication and control with
brain activity only, by interpreting the brain signals, which can be acquired
with an electroencephalogram (EEG) [16]. BCI-based communication technologies could therefore be used as assistive technology for people with physical
impairments in their daily life. Many prototypes for BCI spelling applications
have been developed using various paradigms [1,5,14].

The focus of this paper lies on code modulated visual evoked potentials (c-
VEPs) which are responses to a stimulus of code-modulated sequences [4]. If
the user attends a c-VEP stimuli, the target can be identified through template

© Springer International Publishing AG, part of Springer Nature 2018
J. Ham et al. (Eds.): Symbiotic 2017, LNCS 10727, pp. 53–62, 2018.
https://doi.org/10.1007/978-3-319-91593-7_6

matching with prerecorded data sets. Non-periodic binary code and its different time lags can be used for stimulus modulation. In particular, m-sequences which can be generated using maximal linear feed-back shift registers, are often employed because of their autocorrelation property [3].

In BCI studies, communication speed of BCI spelling interfaces is usually assessed via the information transfer rate (ITR), given in bit per minute (see, e.g., [16]). C-VEP based BCIs have achieved average ITRs around 100 bit/min [4, 11]. Typically, in VEP-based BCIs, stimuli are displayed on standard computer screens. The majority of commercially available monitors is limited to a refresh rate of 60 Hz. Therefore, 60 Hz is typically used in most experimental setups.

The stimuli can be realized as a graphics object (e.g. a box containing a letter) with the binary states drawn/not drawn, which change in dependence of the monitors refresh rate. Thus, the overall speed of the BCI is affected by the refresh rate. For example, for a 60 Hz monitor, the duration of one stimulus cycle using a 63 bit m-sequence is $63/60 = 1.05$ s; a higher refresh rate will decrease the time for one stimulus cycle resulting in potentially higher ITR if accuracy is equal. However, if a higher refresh rate is used, stimuli might be harder to distinguish due to the shorter lag between consecutive targets which could lead to an increased number of classification errors.

This paper investigates different refresh rates for c-VEP based BCIs both in terms of speed and user friendliness. Recently, Aminaka and Rutkowski [2] utilized light-emitting diodes (LEDs) for a command c-VEP system with 31 bit modulation sequence and a relatively high 40 Hz carrier frequency, achieving a grand mean average accuracy of 51%. In our previous studies with steady state visually evoked potentials based BCIs, stimuli of lower frequency (6–12 Hz) have shown to yield high ITRs, but were usually considered slightly more annoying [6,12]. In this study, the level of annoyance associated with each tested refresh rate was assessed with a user questionnaire.

A sixteen command interface was evaluated with monitor refresh rate set to 60 Hz, 120 Hz and 200 Hz, respectively. For stimulus modulation, a 63 bit m-sequence with a lag of 4 bits between stimuli was used. According to Wei et al., who investigated c-VEP parameter setup, these settings yield good performance [15].

2   Methods and Materials

2.1   Participants

Eight healthy volunteers (two women) with a mean age of 27.5 years (standard deviation: 3.7, range: 22–33), participated in the experiment. All had normal or corrected-to-normal vision. The experiment was conducted according to the Helsinki declaration. Before participation, written informed consent in accordance with the Declaration of Helsinki was obtained from all participants. The research was approved by the ethical committee of the medical faculty of the University Duisburg-Essen. Information needed for the analysis of the experiments was stored anonymously during the experiment. Participants had the opportunity to opt-out of the study at any time. Participants did not receive any financial reward for participation.

2.2 Hardware

The participants were seated in front of an LCD screen (Asus ROG Swift PG258Q, resolution: 1920×1080 pixels, maximal vertical refresh rate: 240 Hz), at a distance of about 60 cm. The used computer system operated on Microsoft Windows 7 Enterprise running on an Intel processor (Intel Core i7, 3.40 GHz).

Standard Ag/AgCl electrodes were placed mainly over the visual cortex according to the International 10–20 system (the standard method to describe electrode locations for the EEG recordings). The reference electrode was located at C_Z and the ground electrode at AF_Z. Twelve signal electrodes were used: P_Z, P_3, P_4, PO_3, PO_4, PO_7, PO_8, O_1, O_2, O_Z, O_9, and O_{10}. Standard abrasive electrolytic electrode gel was applied between the electrodes and the scalp to bring impedances below 5 kΩ. An EEG amplifier (g.USBamp, Guger Technologies, Graz, Austria), was utilized. The sampling frequency was set to 600 Hz. During the EEG signal acquisition, an analogue band pass filter (between 2 and 70 Hz) and a notch filter (around 50 Hz) were applied directly in the amplifier.

2.3 Software

M-sequence: For the flashing pattern, we employed so-called m-sequences (see, e.g., [4]) which can be generated using a Linear Feedback Shift Register (LFSR), as displayed in Fig. 1. An LSFR generates a periodic sequence of binary samples. The combination of the register pins can be expressed as mod 2 polynomial:

$$G(X) = X^N + a_{N-1}X^{N-1} + \ldots + a_2X^2 + a_1X + 1, \qquad (1)$$

with $a_i \in \{0,1\}$, $i = 1, \ldots, N-1$ representing the weight of a corresponding register pin and $X^i \in \{0,1\}$, $i = 0, \ldots, N$ the value of a register cell. The length of the generated sequence depends on the values a_i. The maximal length of such sequence is $L = 2^N - 1$. A sequence of maximal length L is called m-sequence, which has an important feature for the design of c-VEP BCIs: The autocorrelation function is 1 at $0, L, 2L, \ldots$, and $1/L$ elsewhere. In this experiment, an LSFR represented by the generator polynom $x^6 + x^5 + 1$ with the initial value 111110 was used to generate a 63 bit m-sequence c_0. By introducing a circular shift τ, one can create a set of m-sequences with shifted autocorrelation functions.

Stimulus Presentation: In this experiment, sixteen 63 bit m-sequences c_i, $i = 0, \ldots, 15$ employing a circular shift of 4 bit between targets were used for stimuli presentation, i.e. c_0 had no shift, c_1 was shifted by 4 bit, c_2 was shifted by 8 bit etc. The stimuli alternated between the binary states 'black' (represented by '0' in the sequence) and 'white' (represented by '1'). The duration for a stimulus cycle in seconds is $T_s = 63/r$ where r represents the monitor refresh rate in Hz. In our experiment, 60 Hz, 120 Hz and 200 Hz were used, leading to 1.05 s, 0.52 s and 0.33 s per cycle, respectively. The time lag τ between two consecutive

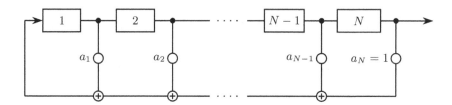

Fig. 1. N-stage Linear Feedback Shift Register (see, e.g., [8] for more details). The register cells hold binary states 1 or 0. Outputs are connected by XOR gates.

targets is $\tau = 4/r$, leading to 0.066 s, 0.033 s and 0.02 s for 60 Hz, 120 Hz and 200 Hz, respectively. Figure 2 illustrates the stimulation sequences used in this experiment.

The targets were arranged as 4×4 matrix, surrounded by 20 non-target stimuli (see Fig. 3). The presentation of the stimuli was synchronized with the amplifier using a trigger channel. An additional box (trigger box, 50×50 pixels) was flashing in the corner of the screen.

A photo transistor (SFH-300, OSRAM Opto Semiconductors, Regensburg, Germany) was placed at the screen at the position of the trigger box. Constant voltage from Voltage divider $V_{in} = 5$ V, $R_1 = 3$ MΩ, $R_2 = 30$ kΩ, $V_{out} = 50$ mV was provided at an additional electrode input (EL_{in}) of the amplifier with the phototransistor connected parallel to the $V_{out} - EL_{in}$ and the ground.

Training: Targets were identified using a template matching method (see, e.g., [4]) which requires a training session. EEG-data of several stimulus cycles of a reference target with underlying code sequence c_0 are recorded, resulting in n_t trials T_i each represented by a $n_c \times n_s$ data matrix, where n_c is the number of channels and n_s is the number of samples. An average template R_0 is obtained by averaging over all recorded training trials T_i. Templates R_k, for all $k = 1, \ldots, K$ targets can be generated by shifting the columns of the template matrix R_0:

$$R_k(j,t) = R_0(j, t - (\tau k)), \quad j = 1, \ldots, n_c, \ \ t = 0, 1, \ldots, n_s, \tag{2}$$

where τ represents the time lag between two consecutive targets. A target that is attended can then be identified by finding the template with maximal correlation to the EEG data recorded during stimulus fixation.

For this purpose and for the design of a spatial filter, canonical-correlation analysis (CCA) was utilized (see, e.g., [7,9]). CCA is a multivariable correlation analysis method that measures the underlying correlation between two multidimensional variables. For two variables X and Y and linear combination $x = X^T W_X$ and $y = Y^T W_Y$, CCA finds weight vectors W_X and W_Y that maximize the correlation ρ between x and y by solving

$$\max_{W_X, W_Y} \rho(x, y) = \frac{E[W_X^T XY^T W_Y]}{\sqrt{E[W_X^T XX^T W_X]E[W_Y^T YY^T W_Y]}}, \tag{3}$$

generating the maximal CCA correlation coefficient $\hat{\rho}(x, y)$. As described by
Spüler et al. [11] a spatial filter is constructed from the training data as follows:

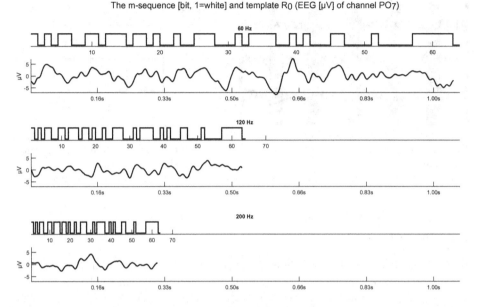

Fig. 2. The modulation sequence c_0 of the reference target and the averaged template
R_0 for the tested monitor refresh rates 60, 120 and 200 Hz.

All trials T_i are concatenated to a matrix X with dimensions $n_c \times (n_t n_s)$.
A matrix S with the same column dimension is constructed by replicating R,
$S = [RR \ldots R]$. X and S are used to obtain the spatial filter W_X by CCA.

For X and S the number of rows (channels) does not need to be the same.
For each participant a leave-one-out cross-validation was performed on the trials
to find the channel that leads to maximal correlation between test data and
template (see [10]).

Classification: The output of the canonical correlation analysis (3), $\hat{\rho}$, can be
used for target identification. The selected command is

$$C = \max_k \hat{\rho}\left(W_X^T Y, R_k\right), \quad k = 1, \ldots, K, \tag{4}$$

where Y refers to the $n_c \times n_s$ signal matrix, containing the multi-channel EEG
signals to the recorded segment of n_s samples that needs to be classified.

In this experiment, the classification methods described above were utilized
on extended time windows. In this respect, a segment Y containing $m n_s$ samples
is classified by replicating W_X, as well as R_k in (4) m times.

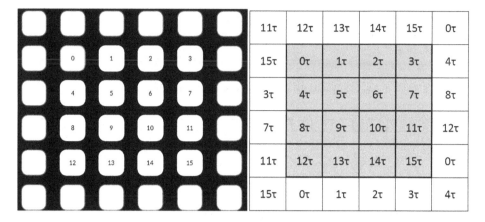

Fig. 3. Graphical user interface of the tested BCI. Sixteen target stimuli and twenty complementary stimuli were presented (total size on the screen was 1000 × 1000 pixels). On the right, the time lag to the reference modulation code is indicated for each target.

2.4 Procedure

Participants sat on a chair facing an LCD screen (at a distance of approximately 60 cm). An EEG cap with passive electrodes was put on and gel was applied until impedances for each signal electrode were below 5 kΩ. Thereafter, the participants were prepared for the EEG recording.

Participants went through three sessions (60, 120 and 200 Hz). Each session consisted of a training phase and a test phase, each presenting target stimuli. In the training phase, each of the sixteen stimuli was attended to for 3.15 s. Depending on the refresh rate, the bit pattern repeated several times during this time window: For the 60 Hz refresh rate, it was repeated three times (3 * 63/60 s), for the 120 Hz setup six times (6 * 63/120 s) and for the 200 Hz session 10 times (10 * 63/200 s). This means, during the training, in total, 48, 96 and 160 trials respectively, were recorded for each setup. The total stimulation duration was equal for each training session (50.4 s).

In the test phase, for each setup, the sixteen targets were attended again in random order. Participants were instructed to fixate the target highlighted by a green frame. After selection, a one second pause was integrated for gaze shifting while the targets did not flicker. To limit fatigue, a five minute break was held between training and test phases as well as between sessions. In the copy spelling phase, the templates obtained in the training session were compared to the raw EEG-signal from all channels.

Results were re-evaluated offline using Matlab environment (Matlab2015b, Massachusetts, USA).

The entire session took approximately one hour for each participant.

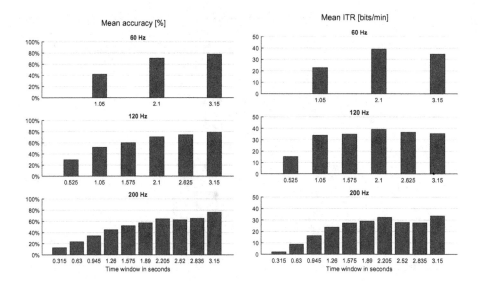

Fig. 4. Mean accuracies and ITRs over all participants. Multiples of the cycle length (0.33 s, 0.52 s and 1.05 s for 60 Hz, 120 Hz and 200 Hz, respectively), where used as classification windows.

Table 1. Accuracies and ITRs for all settings (60 Hz, 120 Hz, and 200 Hz) across all participants. A time window of 3.15 s and a gaze shifting phase of one second was used in all cases. The total time for each test run was 65.4 s.

	60 Hz		120 Hz		200 Hz	
	Acc [%]	ITR [bpm]	Acc [%]	ITR [bpm]	Acc [%]	ITR [bpm]
S1	81.25	37.74	81.25	37.81	68.75	27.99
S2	93.75	50.18	93.75	50.27	87.50	44.12
S3	75.00	32.47	81.25	37.81	93.75	50.82
S4	93.75	50.18	100	58.82	100	59.47
S5	75.00	32.47	62.50	23.24	25.00	3.84
S6	100	58.72	93.75	50.27	93.75	50.82
S7	25.00	3.80	37.50	8.88	62.50	23.50
Mean	77.68	37.94	78.57	38.16	75.89	37.22
SD	23.35	16.72	20.28	16.04	24.42	18.13

3 Results

Performance was evaluated by calculating the commonly used ITR in bits/min (see, e.g., [16]):

$$B = \log_2 N + P \log_2 P + (1 - P) \log_2 \left[\frac{1 - P}{N - 1} \right], \qquad (5)$$

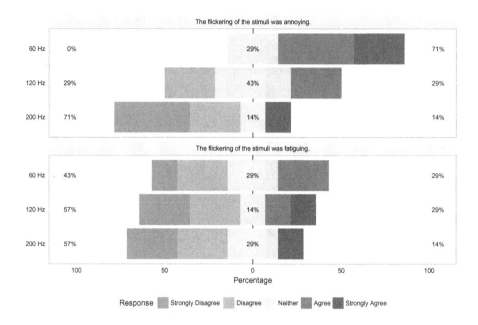

Fig. 5. Results from the user questionaire. Responses were given on a 1-5 Likert scale, 1 indicating strong disagreement and 5 indicating strong agreement.

where, B represents the number of bits per trial. The overall number of possible choices was sixteen ($N = 16$), the accuracy P was calculated based on the number of correct command classifications divided by the total number of classified commands. To obtain ITR in bits per minute, B was multiplied by the number of command classifications per minute.

Figure 5 shows results from the questionnaire. The subjective impressions regarding fatigue level and annoyance were measured using a five-point Likert scale, where "1" indicated the strongest degree of disagreement and "5" the strongest degree of agreement.

One participant, achieved poor results with all refresh rates and was therefore excluded from the analysis presented here. The seven remaining participants achieved a mean accuracies of 77.68%, 78.57%, 75.89% and ITRs of 37.94 bpm, 38.16 bpm and 37.22 bpm for refresh rates of 60, 120 and 200 Hz. Figure 4 and Table 1 summarize results for all participants. Provided are the command accuracy and the ITR for each refresh rate.

4   Discussion

Systems based on stimuli flickering at a higher speed could yield a more user friendly BCI. Although BCI systems utilizing stimuli flickering at a higher speed are usually associated with comparably poor BCI performance [13], in this study, the performance difference with high compared to low refresh rates was surprisingly low. Some participants, e.g. subject 3 and subject 7 achieved best accuracies with the 200 Hz setting. Participant 7 achieved only 25% with the 60 Hz setup but 62.5% with 200 Hz. For participant 5, on the other hand, accuracies for 120 and 200 Hz were poor. Overall, there was surprisingly little performance difference between the tested settings.

Regarding the user friendliness of the systems, most participants seemed to favor the system utilizing the 200 Hz refresh rate (see Fig. 5). The 60 Hz BCI was considered as annoying for the majority of participants. Also in terms of the level of fatigue, the 200 Hz setup yielded best results.

The experiment further demonstrated that larger classification time windows strongly correlate with accuracy (see Fig. 4), which was observed for other VEP-based BCIs as well (see, e.g., [6]).

Acquiring the trigger signal digitally might enhance system performance as well as all signal channels could be used for the EEG acquisition. For each refresh rate the same band pass filter was applied. For the lower refresh rates a narrower bandwidth might improve performance.

The authors would like to note, that a multi target BCI interface, such as presented in this paper, compete with eye tracking interfaces, which allow faster control and are easier to setup. A disadvantage of eye tracking devices is that there is usually no differentiation between intentional and unintentional fixation. Hybrid systems based on eye tracking and BCI that circumvent the issue have been developed [12].

Performance could be improved, if a higher number of electrodes is used; utilizing support vector machines might make the system more robust as well [11]. Future research directions could include sliding time windows for c-VEP online classification. In this study, participants were healthy young adults; tests with a higher number of different participants are planned. Long term studies are necessary to analyze the robustness of the system.

5   Conclusion

In this paper we tested the influence of the monitor refresh rate on c-VEP BCI performance. Data from eight participants were evaluated. Stimuli presentations based on 60, 120 and 200 Hz were tested. The highest refresh rate, 200 Hz, yielded surprisingly good results. Although ITR did drop with increasing refresh rate, the benefits of faster stimuli might outweigh a slightly lower ITR. According to a user questionnaire, the system employing the fastest stimuli was least annoying and fatiguing.

Acknowledgments. This research was supported by the European Fund for Regional Development (EFRD - or EFRE in German) under Grants GE-1-1-047 and IT-1-2-001. We also thank to all the participants of this research study and our student assistants.

References

1. Akce, A., Norton, J.J., Bretl, T.: An SSVEP-based brain-computer interface for text spelling with adaptive queries that maximize information gain rates. IEEE Trans. Neural Syst. Rehabil. Eng. **23**(5), 857–866 (2015)

2. Aminaka, D., Rutkowski, T.M.: A sixteen-command and 40 Hz carrier frequency code-modulated visual evoked potential BCI. In: Guger, C., Allison, B., Lebedev, M. (eds.) Brain-Computer Interface Research. SECE, pp. 97–104. Springer, Cham (2017). https://doi.org/10.1007/978-3-319-64373-1_10

3. Bin, G., Gao, X., Wang, Y., Hong, B., Gao, S.: VEP-based brain-computer interfaces: time, frequency, and code modulations [Research Frontier]. IEEE Comput. Intelli. Mag. **4**(4), 22–26 (2009)

4. Bin, G., Gao, X., Wang, Y., Li, Y., Hong, B., Gao, S.: A high-speed BCI based on code modulation VEP. J. Neural Eng. **8**(2), 025015 (2011)

5. Blankertz, B., Krauledat, M., Dornhege, G., Williamson, J., Murray-Smith, R., Müller, K.-R.: A note on brain actuated spelling with the berlin brain-computer interface. In: Stephanidis, C. (ed.) UAHCI 2007. LNCS, vol. 4555, pp. 759–768. Springer, Heidelberg (2007). https://doi.org/10.1007/978-3-540-73281-5_83

6. Gembler, F., Stawicki, P., Volosyak, I.: Autonomous parameter adjustment for SSVEP-based BCIs with a novel BCI wizard. Front. Neurosci. **9**, 474 (2015)

7. Lin, Z., Zhang, C., Wu, W., Gao, X.: Frequency recognition based on canonical correlation analysis for SSVEP-based BCIs. IEEE Trans. Biomed. Eng. **54**(6), 1172–1176 (2007)

8. Mazurek, R., Lasota, H.: Application of maximum-length sequences to impulse response measurement of hydroacoustic communications systems. Hydroacoustics **10**, 123–130 (2007)

9. Spüler, M., Walter, A., Rosenstiel, W., Bogdan, M.: Spatial filtering based on canonical correlation analysis for classification of evoked or event-related potentials in EEG data. IEEE Trans. Neural Syst. Rehabil. Eng. **22**(6), 1097–1103 (2014)

10. Spüler, M., Rosenstiel, W., Bogdan, M.: One class SVM and canonical correlation analysis increase performance in a c-VEP based Brain-Computer Interface (BCI). In: ESANN (2012)

11. Spüler, M., Rosenstiel, W., Bogdan, M.: Online adaptation of a c-VEP Brain-Computer Interface (BCI) based on error-related potentials and unsupervised learning. PLoS ONE **7**(12), e51077 (2012)

12. Stawicki, P., Gembler, F., Rezeika, A., Volosyak, I.: A novel hybrid mental spelling application based on eye tracking and SSVEP-based BCI. Brain Sci. **7**(4), 35 (2017)

13. Volosyak, I., Cecotti, H., Gräser, A.: Impact of frequency selection on LCD screens for SSVEP based brain-computer interfaces. In: Cabestany, J., Sandoval, F., Prieto, A., Corchado, J.M. (eds.) IWANN 2009. LNCS, vol. 5517, pp. 706–713. Springer, Heidelberg (2009). https://doi.org/10.1007/978-3-642-02478-8_88

14. Volosyak, I., Gembler, F., Stawicki, P.: Age-related differences in SSVEP-based BCI performance. Neurocomputing **250**, 57–64 (2017)

15. Wei, Q., Feng, S., Lu, Z.: Stimulus specificity of brain-computer interfaces based on code modulation visual evoked potentials. PLoS ONE **11**(5), e0156416 (2016)

16. Wolpaw, J., Birbaumer, N., McFarland, D., Pfurtscheller, G., Vaughan, T.: Brain-computer interfaces for communication and control. Clin. Neurophysiol. **113**, 767–791 (2002)

Predicting What You Remember from Brain Activity: EEG-Based Decoding of Long-Term Memory Formation

Taeho Kang[1], Yiyu Chen[1], Siamac Fazli[2], and Christian Wallraven[1(✉)]

[1] Cognitive Systems Lab, Korea University, Seoul, Korea
wallraven@korea.ac.kr
[2] Fraunhofer HHI, Berlin, Germany

Abstract. The use of EEG to enhance learning experience in learning environments can contribute to furthering symbiotic relationship between the user and the system. This study examines whether it is possible to predict successful memorization of previously-learned words in a language learning context from brain activity alone. Participants are tasked with learning German-Korean word association pairs, and their retention performance is tested on the day of and the after learning. We perform statistical analysis as well as single-trial classification to investigate whether brain activity as recorded via multi-channel EEG is able to predict whether a word is remembered or not. Our preliminary results confirm above-chance prediction of successful word learning.

Keywords: BCI · Memory · EEG · Education · Language learning

1 Introduction

Memory is a vital component in language learning & usage [1]. It takes us little effort to recognize the importance of it, seeing how we remember words and their meaning on a daily basis. Imagine if we had a method to determine from our brain activity alone whether new words may be remembered later, or whether a word we had previously learned can be successfully recalled - such a technology would allow for vastly more comfortable, more adaptive, and more successful language learning.

In science, there has been interest in determining whether an individual would remember a piece of information by monitoring brain activities during memory tasks. Given recent developments in both imaging methods (such as fMRI and EEG) as well as statistical analyses, several studies have started to tackle this issue [2–9]. With neuroimaging, for example, studies have shown that the success of memorizing visual experiences can be predicted through brain waves by activations in the prefrontal cortex and the bilateral parahippocampal cortex [2]. For verbal experiences and declarative memory, activity differences in prefrontal and

J. Ham et al. (Eds.): Symbiotic 2017, LNCS 10727, pp. 63–73, 2018.
https://doi.org/10.1007/978-3-319-91593-7_7

temporal cortical areas have been observed between successful and unsuccessful retrievals [3–5]. Similarly, in intracranial EEG studies, cortical increases of power in theta and gamma frequency oscillations have been found for successful subsequent recollection of words [6].

In this study, we aim to further examine the difference between successful and unsuccessful memory formation using scalp EEG in a language learning context. Specifically, we try to characterize potential differences in brain activity between correct and incorrect retrieval right after the learning (encoding), as well as on the day after to investigate aspects of long-term memory formation. In our experiments, participants were to learn words in German and given a memory task in which German-Korean association pairs were to be memorized across several days. During the whole experiment, EEG was recorded, and we employed the EEG data during encoding to predict whether long-term memory of the retention pairs is successfully formed given participants' explicit answers during testing. As we will show, our preliminary results indicate that EEG signals acquired during learning can indeed be used as a predictor for this task.

2 Methods

2.1 Experimental Paradigm

The experiment consisted of two types of sessions: the learning session and the test session as can be shown in Fig. 1. Learning sessions were done to facilitate learning of new words and were comprised of two segments, the encoding segment and the query segment (Fig. 2). In the encoding segment, native Korean speakers with no prior knowledge of German were presented with 60 German words and their respective Korean translation in pairs. When a word was presented for the first time, the pair would be displayed on screen for 5 s. Once the first 10 pairs were presented in this manner, a query segment showing one of the German word without its Korean translation would occur, prompting participants to recall and type the exact Korean translation they were given with a keyboard. If their response matched the translation, a message indicating they were correct would be displayed for 1 s. If their response was incorrect, the correct German-Korean association pair would be displayed again for 5 s.

Each association pair was queried repeatedly-but non-successively-in random order until it was correctly answered 3 times, and then a new word pair would be presented in the same manner as before. Importantly, the brain activity during these queries was used for the analyses reported below. In each query trial, 3 temporal markers were collected (see Fig. 2): when the query was displayed (stimulus onset), when the participant pressed the first key during response (first key-press), and when the participant pressed the final key of the response (response-end). Once querying was done for all 60 word-pairs, the encoding segment would finish and the testing segment would begin.

Finally, in the testing session, the 60 previously learned words would reappear in the same query format, only this time there would not be any feedback of whether their responses were correct or not. The goal of this testing session was

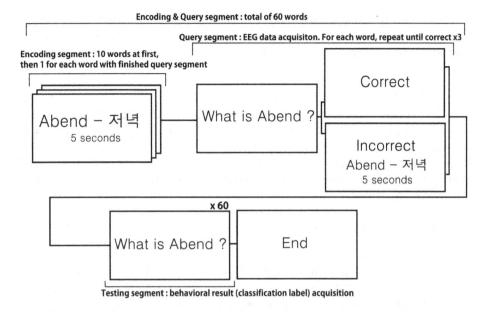

Fig. 1. Visual aid of the experiment paradigm.

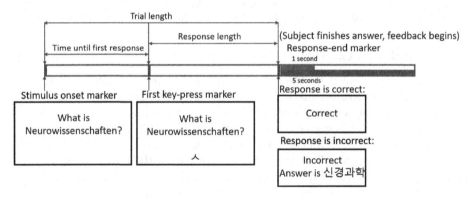

Fig. 2. Visual aid of the trial layout for a query segment with feedback.

to facilitate recollection of information that was learned recently. Importantly, for our analysis, the behavioral result during this session was used as the same-day label as a measure of recall accuracy.

A participant would perform 3 learning sessions and learn 180 new words in this manner per day for a total of 5 days, totaling 900 word association pairs. Starting from the second day, participants performed an additional test session once per day as well. These test sessions were basically a re-iteration of the testing segment from the learning session, only that the last 180 words they had learned from the previous day would be tested instead. This session's goal was to measure long-term recollection of information that was learned longer than 24 h prior. The behavioral results from this test session were used as next-day labels.

To summarize, each participant learned 900 German word pairs, and for each pair there would be two binary labels: same-day and next-day, each representing whether that word was remembered or forgotten during same/next-day tests.

2.2 Participants

A total of 14 participants were recruited for the experiment. All participants were male university students within the 20–30 age bracket ($m = 24.6, s = 1.6$), and were native Korean-speakers who did not have prior knowledge of German. All participants gave informed consents to participating in the experiment and to their data being processed. All participants received compensations for taking part in this experiment.

2.3 EEG Apparatus

For this study, a 63 channel wet electrode EEG was deployed and recorded at a sampling frequency of 1000 Hz. The measured channels were (following MCN notation): EOGv,h,1, F1,5,z,2,6,10, FFT7,8,9, FT9,7,8,10, FC5,3,1,z, 2,4,6, FTT7,8, FCC5,6, T7,8, TTP7,8, TP7,9,8,10, TPP7,8, P3,5,9,z,4,6,10, PO3,7,z,4,8, O1,Oz,O2, CP1,3,5,z,2,4,6, C3,5,z,4,6. All channels were set to sub-10 KΩ impedances before signal measurement. We used ActiCAP electrodes and BrainAmp Amplifier from Brain Products, Germany to acquire EEG signals.

2.4 Stimuli and Coding

For stimuli, a total of 2200 German-Korean word pairs were extracted from a standard German-Korean dictionary published by Doosan-Donga, Korea [10]. Stimuli were displayed on a monitor while the participants were seated. Breaks were inserted to avoid fatigue and to ensure alertness. All sessions of the experiment were conducted in an enclosed, quiet environment.

The experiment paradigm code was written within the Pyff framework [11], operating under Python 2.7.5 for execution and EEG communication. All relevant data from the paradigm was recorded into a SQL file using the SQLite3 library for Python [12].

2.5 Data Analysis

Topographical maps of significant features were calculated by point-biserial correlation coefficients [13]. The point-biserial correlation coefficient is a special case of the Pearson product-moment correlation coefficient used to characterize the association of a binary random variable (in this case 'remembered' and 'forgotten') to a continuous random variable (here channel-wise EEG data). It is defined as:

$$r_{pb} = \frac{M_1 - M_0}{s_n} \sqrt{\frac{n_1 n_0}{n^2}} \quad \text{with} \quad s_n = \sqrt{\frac{1}{n} \sum_{i=1}^{n} (x_i - \bar{x})^2} \tag{1}$$

where x is EEG data values, M_1 and M_0 are the mean values of data points in groups 1 and 0, $n_{1/0}$ the number of examples in groups 1 and 0 and n the total sample size. To ensure normality, correlations were transformed into unit variance z-scores for each participant j using Fisher's z-transform [14] and grand average z-scores were obtained by a weighted sum of individual z-scores over all participants (with $\sqrt{N-3}$ functioning as the weight):

$$z_j = \frac{\tanh^{-1}(r_j)}{\sqrt{m_j - 3}} \quad \text{and} \quad \bar{z} = \frac{\sum_{j=1}^{N} z_j}{\sqrt{N}} \tag{2}$$

where m_j is the sample size of participant j and $N = 14$ the total number of participants. p-values for the hypothesis of zero correlation in the grand average were computed by means of a two-sided z-test. All reported p-values were Bonferroni-corrected for the number of channels times the number of time points, to account for multiple hypothesis testing [15].

Raw EEG signals were filtered at a pass band of [0.5 40]Hz, and downsampled to 100 Hz. Channels with impedance over 50 mΩ were rejected. To characterize brain activity during long-term memory formation, we used an event-related-potential analysis. For stimulus-locked ERPs, epochs were created at [−200 1000] ms in relation to stimulus onset. Eye-movement artifact rejections were done by finding trials in which maximum-minimum amplitudes at a window of [200 1000] ms exceeded 150 μV in any of the two EOG channels. Variance-based rejection was also performed, and baseline-correction was applied with respect to an interval of [−200 0] ms. For response-locked ERPs, epochs were created at [−1200 200] ms with regard to the first key-press marker, which was defined as the beginning of the typed response. The same max-min artifact rejection was applied with 150 μV at a window of [−1000 −0] ms. There were a total of 49244 epoch samples before artifact rejection was done. After rejections were done there were 26865 epoch samples for stimulus-locked and 14959 samples for response-locked.

Next, single-trial classification prediction was done with regularized linear discrimination algorithm (RLDA) on preprocessed EEG epochs. 10 fold cross-validation with 10 splits was performed to ensure generalizability of the results. In order to calculate the features, the stimulus-locked EEG epochs of [−200 1000] ms were used, with EOG channels removed. Stimulus-locked ERP epochs were first truncated across time for every 10 time values, then divided into pre-stimulus epochs ([−200 0] ms) and post-stimulus epochs ([200 1000] ms). For both pre and post stimulus epochs, classification was done for same-day and next-day, each trained in datasets that were not balanced for each class and in datasets that had even number of trials in each class (balanced) on different instances. Within these smaller intervals the time dimension was averaged. Both the analysis and the classification were based on the same preprocessed data. As metrics for classification learning quality, participant mean accuracy levels for overall correct predictions for both classes with standard error of mean, and precision & recall rates for the remembered class were calculated. Above chance level for prediction was determined by assessing the lower bound of the participant mean accuracy accounting for the standard error of mean.

3   Results

3.1   Behavioral Result

Each trial had three markers: the onset of one word question stimulus, the first key press response of the participant, and the last key press of the participant. In total 49244 trials were collected across 14 participants. For tests done at the day of the learning (same-day), participants correctly remembered $78.7\%(s = 13.0)$ of the words encountered on average. On tests done 24 h after the learning (next-day), participants achieved a mean performance of $37.6\%(s = 17.1)$. Best and worst performing participants had 96.2% and 51.2% accuracy for same-day, and 79.8% and 12.4% for next-day tests. The performance drop was highly significant as shown by a paired t-test $(t(13) = 13.16, p < .001)$, showing that an additional day hurt long-term memory recall. A correlation between participants' same-day and next-day test performance was found $(r = 0.77, p < 0.01)$, indicating that performance across days was highly consistent within the same participant.

Next, we looked at reaction times, defined as the time to the first key press. A participant-wise median comparison of this duration between trials from remembered and forgotten pairs was performed, and on average the response began $555.6\,\mathrm{ms}(s = 190.8)$ earlier in remembered trials than in forgotten trials under same-day labels, and $531.2\,\mathrm{ms}(s = 190.8)$ earlier in remembered trials under next-day labels. A paired t-test of the median reaction times across participants was significant for both same and next day labels $(t(13) = -10.89, p < .001$, and $t(13) = 9.10, p < .001)$, showing that responses were consistently faster for the remembered trials. In line with the previous results, correlations between remembered and forgotten trials showed highly consistent reaction time behavior for both day-labels as well: $(r = 0.95, p < .001)$, and $(r = 0.90, p < .001)$.

3.2   Signal Analysis Result

Stimulus-locked ERP results were analyzed first. Figure 3a, b show the scalp-wide plot of averaged statistical significance (signed log p) obtained by comparing between signals from remembered and forgotten trials, on same-day and next-day labels respectively for each row. Significant features are marked by bold contour lines. In both cases using same-day and next-day labels, a significant difference between trials from remembered and forgotten words is visible around 600 ms post stimulus. Significance levels for the next-day labels are weaker compared to those obtained on the same day. The overall dynamics start with a somewhat right-lateralized temporal activation that very quickly spreads out to a whole-scalp pattern, persisting until 1000 ms after stimulus onset.

Since we found marked reaction time differences between remembered and forgotten words (see above), the observed ERP differences may simply be due to

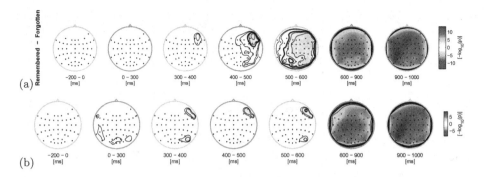

Fig. 3. Scalp-wide plot of averaged statistical significance (signed log p) comparing between stimulus-locked signals from remembered and forgotten trials on same-day and next-day labels. First row shows signed log-p values created from comparing remembered and forgotten trial signals using same-day test results as the label, and the second row from using next-day test results.

differences in response onset. For this reason, we next looked at response-locked ERP results obtained by extracting epochs in relation to the time of first keypress at [−1200 ms 200 ms]. For this analysis around 9% of all trials for which response times were shorter than 1200 ms were discarded. Plots of statistical significance for response-locked ERP in the same format as before can be seen in Fig. 4a,b. Here as well, in both same and next-day labels a significant positive difference between remembered and forgotten trials were found, this time around 600 ms to 200 ms before the behavioral response began. The timing of peak differences is slightly different for the same and next-day labels, however, with the next-day pattern starting somewhat earlier. Here, we see both central and right-lateralized temporal activation that starts out with a more centralized activation during the peak compared to the stimulus-locked ERP results (Fig. 3a, b).

3.3   Classification Result

Classification for same-day labels are shown on Table 1 and next-day labels on Table 2. In each table, results from classification using datasets right after preprocessing (i.e. without balancing samples for classes) are shown outside brackets, with results from classification with datasets in which trials numbers were balanced inside the brackets. For pre-stimulus same-day labels, above-chance level classification accuracy levels were found in 12 out of 14 participants unbalanced datasets and 4 out of 14 in balanced datasets. In post-stimulus same-day labels, 12 out of 14 participants had above chance level accuracies in unbalanced, and also 12 out of 14 in balanced datasets. Under next-day labels, unbalanced pre-stimulus data from 8 out of 14 participants were indicative of above chance predictions, with 8 out of 14 participants having above chance predictions in balanced datasets as well. For post-stimulus next-day labels, 10 out of 14 participants' data were found to be predictive above chance with unbalanced data,

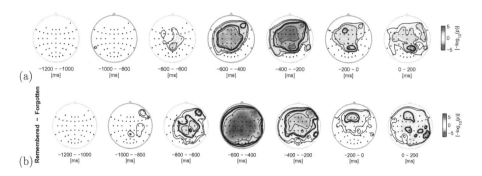

Fig. 4. Scalp-wide plot of averaged statistical significance (signed log p) comparing between response-locked signals from remembered and forgotten trials on same-day and next-day labels. First row shows signed log-p values created from comparing remembered and forgotten trial signals using same-day test results as the label, and the second row from using next-day test results.

Table 1. Single trial classification results for pre- and post-stimulus ERP data. Labels are either extracted from the Same-day testing session. Numbers in the brackets denote classification results from balanced datasets, while the numbers outside show classification results from datasets without balancing.

Subj.	Pre-stimulus			Post-stimulus		
	Accuracy	Precision	Recall	Accuracy	Precision	Recall
sbj1	56.1 ± 3.2 {49.1 ± 3.8}	0.77 {0.48}	0.56 {0.34}	49.8 ± 3.2 {58.1 ± 3.8}	0.70 {0.59}	0.52 {0.61}
sbj2	50.8 ± 1.1 {54.3 ± 1.0}	0.39 {0.54}	0.48 {0.60}	52.4 ± 1.1 {54.7 ± 1.0}	0.40 {0.55}	0.50 {0.53}
sbj3	57.2 ± 1.7 {52.3 ± 3.3}	0.92 {0.52}	0.59 {0.55}	68.1 ± 1.7 {57.9 ± 3.3}	0.93 {0.61}	0.70 {0.51}
sbj4	58.6 ± 1.0 {50.0 ± 2.2}	0.81 {0.49}	0.64 {0.52}	59.8 ± 1.0 {53.2 ± 2.2}	0.82 {0.53}	0.65 {0.56}
sbj5	63.6 ± 2.0 {48.5 ± 3.0}	0.85 {0.48}	0.70 {0.54}	65.6 ± 2.0 {54.9 ± 3.0}	0.86 {0.56}	0.71 {0.56}
sbj6	50.9 ± 1.3 {46.4 ± 1.4}	0.61 {0.46}	0.59 {0.47}	54.0 ± 1.3 {54.2 ± 1.4}	0.66 {0.55}	0.55 {0.52}
sbj7	52.5 ± 1.0 {50.9 ± 1.2}	0.66 {0.51}	0.56 {0.53}	56.2 ± 1.0 {55.6 ± 1.2}	0.70 {0.56}	0.58 {0.57}
sbj8	56.4 ± 1.7 {55.6 ± 2.3}	0.79 {0.56}	0.59 {0.56}	56.6 ± 1.7 {55.0 ± 2.3}	0.78 {0.56}	0.62 {0.54}
sbj9	54.2 ± 2.2 {49.1 ± 2.4}	0.83 {0.50}	0.57 {0.54}	61.3 ± 2.2 {52.3 ± 2.4}	0.84 {0.51}	0.67 {0.54}
sbj10	57.3 ± 1.0 {53.2 ± 1.6}	0.78 {0.53}	0.62 {0.54}	56.2 ± 1.0 {54.4 ± 1.6}	0.79 {0.54}	0.59 {0.54}
sbj11	60.5 ± 0.8 {45.8 ± 2.2}	0.89 {0.46}	0.64 {0.48}	64.2 ± 0.8 {56.0 ± 2.2}	0.91 {0.57}	0.67 {0.51}
sbj12	52.0 ± 1.9 {53.1 ± 1.6}	0.67 {0.54}	0.54 {0.51}	49.8 ± 1.9 {56.5 ± 1.6}	0.64 {0.56}	0.53 {0.59}
sbj13	51.3 ± 1.0 {48.9 ± 0.8}	0.56 {0.49}	0.55 {0.50}	54.6 ± 1.0 {58.3 ± 0.8}	0.60 {0.58}	0.54 {0.57}
sbj14	65.6 ± 1.5 {53.3 ± 4.2}	0.96 {0.52}	0.67 {0.53}	74.0 ± 1.5 {52.4 ± 4.2}	0.96 {0.53}	0.76 {0.48}

with 13 out of 14 participant datasets showing above-chance level predictions in balanced datasets.

4   Discussion and Conclusions

Through this study, we have examined the difference in measured neurophysiological signals between remembered and forgotten information during language learning. Our findings are in line with previous studies [3–5] in that there are significant differences between the two conditions.

Table 2. Single trial classification results for pre- and post-stimulus ERP data. Labels are either extracted from the Next-day testing session. Numbers in the brackets denote classification results from balanced datasets, while the numbers outside show classification results from datasets without balancing.

Subj.	Pre-stimulus			Post-stimulus		
	Accuracy	Precision	Recall	Accuracy	Precision	Recall
sbj1	54.0 ± 2.4 {57.3 ± 5.3}	0.32 {0.62}	0.39 {0.54}	48.9 ± 2.4 {52.0 ± 5.3}	0.25 {0.52}	0.37 {0.53}
sbj2	69.8 ± 0.9 {53.0 ± 2.9}	0.05 {0.54}	0.27 {0.59}	76.4 ± 0.9 {53.0 ± 2.9}	0.09 {0.52}	0.32 {0.57}
sbj3	50.4 ± 1.1 {51.7 ± 0.7}	0.61 {0.52}	0.55 {0.55}	52.7 ± 1.1 {53.3 ± 0.7}	0.65 {0.54}	0.51 {0.52}
sbj4	49.0 ± 1.8 {51.4 ± 1.3}	0.24 {0.52}	0.43 {0.51}	57.6 ± 1.8 {54.9 ± 1.3}	0.31 {0.55}	0.48 {0.58}
sbj5	54.2 ± 2.1 {52.1 ± 1.7}	0.27 {0.52}	0.31 {0.54}	56.2 ± 2.1 {57.1 ± 1.7}	0.32 {0.56}	0.42 {0.63}
sbj6	56.9 ± 1.0 {48.6 ± 2.3}	0.19 {0.49}	0.44 {0.59}	57.7 ± 1.0 {54.6 ± 2.3}	0.20 {0.54}	0.47 {0.57}
sbj7	53.8 ± 0.5 {52.0 ± 1.4}	0.27 {0.52}	0.41 {0.55}	55.1 ± 0.5 {55.3 ± 1.4}	0.29 {0.56}	0.47 {0.53}
sbj8	55.5 ± 2.2 {45.1 ± 2.2}	0.18 {0.46}	0.40 {0.50}	56.4 ± 2.2 {54.1 ± 2.2}	0.18 {0.53}	0.36 {0.54}
sbj9	47.7 ± 1.5 {54.5 ± 2.9}	0.26 {0.56}	0.44 {0.60}	55.2 ± 1.5 {55.7 ± 2.9}	0.32 {0.55}	0.45 {0.54}
sbj10	51.3 ± 0.5 {53.1 ± 1.0}	0.47 {0.53}	0.49 {0.52}	53.9 ± 0.5 {54.8 ± 1.0}	0.50 {0.55}	0.52 {0.54}
sbj11	49.7 ± 1.3 {49.9 ± 1.1}	0.41 {0.50}	0.49 {0.56}	51.7 ± 1.3 {55.3 ± 1.1}	0.43 {0.56}	0.46 {0.52}
sbj12	50.1 ± 1.4 {50.0 ± 1.0}	0.36 {0.50}	0.49 {0.48}	47.5 ± 1.4 {54.3 ± 1.0}	0.33 {0.55}	0.45 {0.55}
sbj13	55.4 ± 0.8 {49.8 ± 1.4}	0.21 {0.50}	0.34 {0.52}	60.2 ± 0.8 {54.6 ± 1.4}	0.28 {0.55}	0.46 {0.54}
sbj14	49.4 ± 1.2 {50.3 ± 1.3}	0.76 {0.50}	0.52 {0.56}	54.9 ± 1.2 {52.8 ± 1.3}	0.80 {0.53}	0.57 {0.51}

Despite the significance, this observation alone is not sufficient to conclude that what we have seen here is due solely to memory-based brain activation in the retrieval process. Especially for the stimulus-locked analysis, results could have been confounded by the fact that participants were allowed to take their time before formulating a behavioral response - hence, there presumably was considerable variability in the timing of the successful retrieval process. The pattern we saw could therefore be simply due to the differences in reaction time we saw from the behavioral responses - that is, the remembered trials were consistently faster than the forgotten ones, which could have resulted in several large-scale brain activation patterns, such as readiness potentials for initiating motor responses (such as typing the words), etc.

In lieu of this, we deemed it necessary to look into response-locked ERPs as well. Although the first key-press may not be the definitive start of participants' behavioral responses, it is likely that the "a-ha" moment closely precedes the start of response, and would therefore have less varying temporal distance from the marker. Given that our response-locked ERPs did, indeed, also show significant differences between the two conditions as well, it's strongly possible that the markers of memory retrieval process is apparent in our results. Yet, this is still insufficient to conclude what we observed can be solely attributed to brain activity. Somewhat owing to their non-invasiveness, EEG signals are especially susceptible to artifacts such as eye and muscular movement, and though there are methods available to remove artifact signals, isolating brain signals from such noise is a difficult task. We believe further study could be done in acquiring muscular movement signals such as EMGs to investigate the possibility of dissociating the effect of muscle movements from such signals.

It should also be noted that, unlike some of the previous studies, our results have most if not all of the scalp region marked as significant, in a burst form (see Fig. 4a, b). Since EEG analysis - and especially ERP analysis - is much more prone to noise and movement artifacts compared to its invasive counterparts, we tried to run varying configurations for artifact rejection with different rejection thresholds and critical period lengths for the ERP analysis as well. At our most strict threshold of $75\,\mu V$ (compared to the $150\,\mu V$ used for reporting the results above), the "burst" form in scalp plots persisted in a similar pattern, but due to the fact that stricter criteria drastically reduced the number of available trials to work with, we do not report the results here in detail.

Concerning the differences in brain pattern, it should also be noted that our experimental paradigm is different from those used in prior studies. In these, familiarity tests were often employed to facilitate recollection, whereas ours required the participant to recall the queried information completely. It should also be noted that the test of recollection in our study was done both on the day of and after learning, effectively testing recollection at different times. For both times, we did find largely consistent brain patterns in the grand average data. For a better understanding of the brain activation underlying successful learning and retrieval from long-term memory, we will next look into connectivity and source localization, as well as different analysis methods such as oscillatory components (that is, spectral analysis).

While the accuracy of recollection prediction is not yet reliable enough, we did find above-chance decoding accuracy for the 13 out of 14 participants. Additional improvement will come from more advanced analysis pipelines, such as common spatial patterns (CSPs) or newer deep-learning methods that hold promise given the large number of trials that were done in our paradigm. With this, we think that our approach has considerable potential in application. Knowing the important role memory formation plays in human learning, there will be considerable merit in deploying memory prediction as a method of student learning augmentation in the education industry. As of now, learner assessment through BCI technology is an untold story. Studies have emphasized the importance of tutor feedbacks and student diagnostics in tutoring [16,17]. In this domain, intelligent tutoring systems have still vast room for improvement compared to human counterparts. BCI can greatly assist in that domain by providing more empirical data than other conventional means, and being able to predict whether a student may remember a piece of information in the future would be a highly significant outcome.

Acknowledgment. This work was supported by Institute for Information & Communications Technology Promotion (IITP) grant funded by the Korea government (No. 2017-0-00451). This publication only reflects the authors views.

References

1. Ullman, M.T.: Contributions of memory circuits to language: the declarative/procedural model. Cognition **92**(1), 231–270 (2004)
2. Brewer, J.B., Zhao, Z., Desmond, J.E., Glover, G.H., Gabrieli, J.D.E.: Making memories: brain activity that predicts how well visual experience will be remembered. Science **281**(5380), 1185–1187 (1998)
3. Wagner, A.D., Schacter, D.L., Rotte, M., Koutstaal, W., Maril, A., Dale, A.M., Rosen, B.R., Buckner, R.L.: Building memories: remembering and forgetting of verbal experiences as predicted by brain activity. Science **281**(5380), 1188–1191 (1998)
4. Paller, K.A., Wagner, A.D.: Observing the transformation of experience into memory. Trends Cogn. Sci. **6**(2), 93–102 (2002)
5. Kim, H.: Neural activity that predicts subsequent memory and forgetting: a meta-analysis of 74 fMRI studies. Neuroimage **54**(3), 2446–2461 (2011)
6. Sederberg, P.B., Kahana, M.J., Howard, M.W., Donner, E.J., Madsen, J.R.: Theta and gamma oscillations during encoding predict subsequent recall. J. Neurosci. **23**(34), 10809–10814 (2003)
7. Takashima, A., Petersson, K.M., Rutters, F., Tendolkar, I., Jensen, O., Zwarts, M., McNaughton, B., Fernandez, G.: Declarative memory consolidation in humans: a prospective functional magnetic resonance imaging study. Proc. Natl. Acad. Sci. US Am. **103**(3), 756–761 (2006)
8. Long, N.M., Kahana, M.J.: Successful memory formation is driven by contextual encoding in the core memory network. NeuroImage **119**, 332–337 (2015)
9. Osipova, D., Takashima, A., Oostenveld, R., Fernández, G., Maris, E., Jensen, O.: Theta and gamma oscillations predict encoding and retrieval of declarative memory. J. Neurosci. **26**(28), 7523–7531 (2006)
10. Doosan-Donga, co.: Prime German-Korean dictionary, concise version (2010)
11. Venthur, B., Blankertz, B.: A platform-independent open-source feedback framework for BCI systems. In: Proceedings of the 4th International Brain-Computer Interface Workshop and Training Course 2008, Verlag der Technischen Universitt Graz (2008)
12. SQLite: The Database at the Edge of the Network with Dr. Richard Hipp (2015)
13. Tate, R.F.: Correlation between a discrete and a continuous variable. Point-biserial correlation. Ann. Math. Stat. **25**(3), 603–607 (1954)
14. Hotelling, H.: New light on the correlation coefficient and its Transforms. J. Royal Stat. Soci. Ser. B (Methodological) **15**(2), 193–232 (1953)
15. Bonferroni, C.E.: Teoria statistica delle classi e calcolo delle probabilita. Libreria internazionale Seeber (1936)
16. VanLehn, K.: The relative effectiveness of human tutoring, intelligent tutoring systems, and other tutoring systems. Educ. Psychol. **46**(4), 197–221 (2011)
17. Merrill, D.C., Reiser, B.J., Ranney, M., Trafton, J.G.: Effective tutoring techniques: a comparison of human tutors and intelligent tutoring systems. J. Learn. Sci. **2**(3), 277–305 (1992)

Towards a Conceptual Framework
for Cognitive Probing

Laurens R. Krol$^{(\boxtimes)}$ and Thorsten O. Zander

Biological Psychology and Neuroergonomics,
Technische Universität Berlin, Berlin, Germany
lrkrol@gmail.com

Abstract. Cognitive probing combines the ability of computers to interpret ongoing measures of arbitrary brain activity, with the ability of those same computers to actively elicit cognitive responses from their users. Purposefully elicited responses can be interpreted in order to learn about the user, enable symbiotic and implicit interaction, and support neuroadaptive technology. We propose a working definition of cognitive probing that allows it to be generalised across different applications and disciplines.

Keywords: Cognitive probing · Brain-computer interface
Neuroadaptive technology · Implicit interaction
Human-computer interaction

1 Introduction

A brain-computer interface (BCI) is a system that allows an output channel to be established directly between a user's brain and a technological system—an output channel "that is neither neuromuscular nor hormonal" [9]. This allows for example completely paralysed or locked-in patients to communicate with the outside world using mental spellers [1] or brain-activated prostheses [7]. Through BCI systems, people can control such devices using only their brain activity.

A *passive* brain-computer interface (pBCI) [14] uses similar hard- and software in order to interpret brain activity that was not meant to control a device. Instead, it detects and interprets "natural" [5] brain activity that reflects the user's cognitive and mental state, and uses this as *implicit input* to support ongoing human-computer interaction [12].

The automatic correction of user response errors is an early example of what is now known as pBCI. For example in a speeded reaction task, whenever an error negativity [3] was detected, the response would be undone [8]. This approach was later extended to machine errors: whenever the user observed the machine committing an error, it could be corrected if the appropriate brain signal was detected [13].

Note that these are indeed passive BCI applications, since the perception of such an error itself elicits the relevant brain activity, and the user expends no additional effort to inform the computer of the fact that an error occurred.

That machine errors elicit such a detectable response, confirmed also by other experiments [2], is a fact that can be actively exploited by the system. For example, the system can tentatively perform any number of random acts, and can then assess, using pBCI, whether or not these were perceived as erroneous or not by the user. Any action that was not perceived to be in error can then be definitively committed. As such, the user would have implicitly communicated to the system what they wanted it to do, without having given any explicit commands or instructions [11].

Such a scenario was recently demonstrated to be possible using a form of implicit cursor control [11,15], and separately by another group using a robotic arm [4]. In this paper, we take the former as an example. Participants were observing the initially random movements of a cursor on a grid, on which one target location was indicated. For each movement, the computer could assess from ongoing measurements of brain activity whether or not that movement was perceived as either "acceptable" or "not acceptable". Using this information, the system learned over time which movements were apparently desired by the user, and adapted the cursor's behaviour in order to steer it towards the target location.

We believe that this approach, where the computer purposefully elicits responses in order to obtain information not explicitly communicated by the user, can be formulated more generally. The approach is not unique to the above-mentioned example: armed with a general formulation we can see, in retrospect, that other, older applications have used this method as well. A standard definition of this approach should make it more easily recognisable as such, highlighting it as a worthwhile method of its own, and making it more accessible to other researchers across disciplines. We propose to name this approach *cognitive probing*.

2   Cognitive Probing

Cognitive probing refers to the general use of this approach. A stricter definition focuses on the defining behaviour of the system at hand: such a system utilises *cognitive probes*. We propose the following definition of a cognitive probe:

A cognitive probe is a single autogenous system adaptation that is initiated or co-opted by that system in order to learn from the user's contextual, cognitive brain response to it.

This definition consists of a number of terms that may warrant further discussion.

First of all, we use the term *system adaptation* to refer to any state change of the technological system [5,6], be they the perceptible presentation of stimuli or feedback, or more subtle changes to the state or behaviour of the system.

One such state change is *autogenous* when it is initiated by the system. This separates cognitive probes from adaptations whose specific form was decided by the human user, for example through explicit commands.

Such an autogenous state change can be either intended to be a probe—i.e. *initiated* primarily for that purpose—or, it can be a state change that occurs primarily for other reasons, for example, the presentation of feedback to inform the user. Such a latter adaptation may however still elicit a detectable brain response, can thus still be used for the same purpose—i.e., it can be *co-opted* to serve as a probe.

We are focusing in this definition on the user's *cognitive brain response* to these adaptations, as inferred from measures of their brain activity. The probes must thus in one way or another elicit cognition-related brain activity, or a change in ongoing brain activity.

Ultimately, the goal of cognitive probing is to obtain information from the user's brain response to the probes, either about the user, about a specific adaptation, or about the system as a whole. In short, the probes serve to *learn*.

For the gathered information to be meaningfully used as a basis for learning, further information is required. Not only the response itself must be known, but also, what elicited that response. That is the minimum possible *context* of the brain response. However, this context can be extended further to include other relevant contextual aspects: for example, the response may be dependent of the time of day, the physical location, or any other number of situational aspects.

3   Discussion

The example mentioned in the introduction fits the proposed definition of cognitive probing in the following way. Each single cursor movement was initiated by the computer itself, with the goal of eliciting a specific brain response. This response was then recorded in a user model that described the inferred user preferences in relation to the different possible movement directions. The system thus learned the user's preferred cursor behaviour. The observed improvement in the cursor's performance [15] demonstrates the effectiveness of this approach. In particular, the approach implemented here makes use of a sequence of probes. Where traditional BCI applications often use direct (open-loop or closed-loop [5]) adaptations based directly on single-trial brain responses, this example shows how multiple probes from a known context, combined with their (implicit) brain responses, can lead to inferences of higher aspects of cognition, in this case the desired cursor behaviour.

Note that the system could have learned this information even if the cursor continued to move randomly. However, the cursor used the obtained information in real time in order to reach its goal more quickly. This neuroadaptive behaviour of the cursor is not a necessity according to the proposed definition, although it illustrates how this approach can be used to increase the interactivity of human-computer interaction, based entirely on implicitly communicated information [5,11]. Such interactions based on implicit input can provide the basis for a close, symbiotic relationship between humans and technology.

In the real world, we must deal not only with noisy environments, but also with a rich, uncontrollable context. Importantly, because the learning is based on implicit information and can be extended over longer periods of time, the single-trial accuracy of the system is not as critical as it would be for any sort of direct control application. Thus, this approach can be effective even with sub-perfect acquisition technology, such as more user-friendly dry electrodes [10]. Furthermore, even in varying environments and contexts, the primary context of interest is always known—it is the probe itself. Any contextual information that is added may be helpful, but is not required.

Because of this, we believe cognitive probing to be a promising strategy to be used for next-generation neuroadaptive technology, provided that it is used with due consideration and respect for the user's privacy of thought.

Acknowledgements. Part of this work was supported by the Deutsche Forschungs-gemeinschaft (ZA 821/3-1).

References

1. Birbaumer, N., Ghanayim, N., Hinterberger, T., Iversen, I., Kotchoubey, B., Kübler, A., Perelmouter, J., Taub, E., Flor, H.: A spelling device for the paralysed. Nature **398**(6725), 297–298 (1999)
2. Chavarriaga, R., Sobolewski, A., Millán, J.D.R.: Errare machinale est: the use of error-related potentials in brain-machine interfaces. Front. Neurosci. **8**, 208 (2014). https://doi.org/10.3389/fnins.2014.00208
3. Falkenstein, M., Hoormann, J., Christ, S., Hohnsbein, J.: ERP components on reaction errors and their functional significance: a tutorial. Biol. Psychol. **51**(2–3), 87–107 (2000)
4. Iturrate, I., Chavarriaga, R., Montesano, L., Minguez, J., Millán, J.D.R.: Teaching brain-machine interfaces as an alternative paradigm to neuroprosthetics control. Sci. Rep. **5**, 13893 (2015). https://doi.org/10.1038/srep13893
5. Krol, L.R., Andreessen, L.M., Zander, T.O.: Passive brain-computer interfaces: a perspective on increased interactivity. In: Nam, C.S., Nijholt, A., Lotte, F. (eds.) Brain-Computer Interfaces Handbook: Technological and Theoretical Advances, pp. 69–86. CRC Press, Boca Raton (2018)
6. Krol, L.R., Zander, T.O.: Passive BCI-based neuroadaptive systems. In: Proceedings of the 7th Graz Brain-Computer Interface Conference 2017, pp. 248–253 (2017)
7. Müller-Putz, G.R., Pfurtscheller, G.: Control of an electrical prosthesis with an SSVEP-based BCI. IEEE Trans. Biomed. Eng. **55**(1), 361–364 (2008)
8. Parra, L.C., Spence, C.D., Gerson, A.D., Sajda, P.: Response error correction—a demonstration of improved human-machine performance using real-time EEG monitoring. IEEE Trans. Neural Syst. Rehabil. Eng. **11**(2), 173–177 (2003)
9. Wolpaw, J.R., Wolpaw, E.W.: Brain-computer interfaces: something new under the sun. In: Wolpaw, J.R., Wolpaw, E.W. (eds.) Brain-Computer Interfaces: Principles and Practice, pp. 3–12. Oxford University Press, Oxford (2012). https://doi.org/10.1093/acprof:oso/9780195388855.003.0001
10. Zander, T.O., Andreessen, L.M., Berg, A., Bleuel, M., Pawlitzki, J., Zawallich, L., Krol, L.R., Gramann, K.: Evaluation of a dry EEG system for application of passive brain-computer interfaces in autonomous driving. Front. Hum. Neurosci. **11**, 78 (2017). https://doi.org/10.3389/fnhum.2017.00078

11. Zander, T.O., Brönstrup, J., Lorenz, R., Krol, L.R.: Towards BCI-based implicit control in human–computer interaction. In: Fairclough, S.H., Gilleade, K. (eds.) Advances in Physiological Computing. HIS, pp. 67–90. Springer, London (2014). https://doi.org/10.1007/978-1-4471-6392-3_4

12. Zander, T.O., Kothe, C.A.: Towards passive brain-computer interfaces: applying brain-computer interface technology to human-machine systems in general. J. Neural Eng. 8(2), 025005 (2011). https://doi.org/10.1088/1741-2560/8/2/025005

13. Zander, T.O., Kothe, C.A., Jatzev, S., Dashuber, R., Welke, S., De Filippis, M., Rötting, M.: Team PhyPA: developing applications for brain-computer interaction. In: Proceedings of the Brain-Computer Interfaces for HCI and Games Workshop at the SIGCHI Conference on Human Factors in Computing Systems (CHI) (2008)

14. Zander, T.O., Kothe, C.A., Welke, S., Rötting, M.: Enhancing human-machine systems with secondary input from passive brain-computer interfaces. In: Proceedings of the 4th International Brain-Computer Interface Workshop & Training Course, pp. 144–149. Verlag der Technischen Universität Graz, Graz (2008)

15. Zander, T.O., Krol, L.R., Birbaumer, N.P., Gramann, K.: Neuroadaptive technology enables implicit cursor control based on medial prefrontal cortex activity. Proc. Natl. Acad. Sci. 113(52), 14898–14903 (2016)

Human-Aware Navigation
for Autonomous Mobile Robots
for Intra-factory Logistics

Francisco Marques[1]([✉]), Duarte Gonçalves[1], José Barata[1],
and Pedro Santana[2,3]

[1] CTS-UNINOVA, Universidade Nova de Lisboa (UNL), Lisbon, Portugal
fam@uninova.pt
[2] Instituto Universitário de Lisboa (ISCTE-IUL), Lisbon, Portugal
pedro.santana@iscte-iul.pt
[3] Instituto de Telecomunicações (IT), Lisbon, Portugal

Abstract. This paper presents a human-aware navigation system for
mobile robots targeted to cooperative assembly in intra-factory logistics
scenarios. To improve overall efficiency of the operator-robot ensemble,
assembly stations and operators are modelled as cost functions in a layered cost map supporting the robot navigation system. At each new sensory update, the system uses each operator's estimated location to affect
the cost map accordingly. To promote predictability and comfort in the
human operator, the cost map is affected according to the Proxemics
theory, properly adapted to take into account the layout activity space
of the station in which the operator is working. Knowledge regarding
which task and station are being handled by the operator are assumed
to be given to the robot by the factory's computational infrastructure.
To foster integration in existing robots, the system is implemented on
top of the navigation system of the Robot Operating System (ROS).

Keywords: Navigation · Human-aware · Autonomous navigation
Manufacturing systems · Intra-factory logistics

1 Introduction

Nowadays, robotics is ubiquitous on almost all industries. However, given the
ever increasing need for diversification and customization of products and services, a new wave of flexible and more collaborative robots are being introduced
into the shop floor. The goal is to have fenceless environments where robots and
operators can collaborate to increase the efficiency of assembly tasks.

Robots in manufacturing are expanding from more traditional operations, as welding and painting, to factory intra-logistics [9] and collaborative assembly [12]. These new tasks demand for a shift in the human-robot
interaction paradigm in manufacturing, where robots need to adapt to their
humans counterparts and not the other way around. Although more and more

autonomous mobile robots are specifically designed for shop floors [1, 6, 15], their navigation systems are still not fully tuned for this new approach.

Despite the fact that human-awareness in robot navigation tasks has been considerably studied for office environments, museums, and households [7], in the manufacturing domain human-awareness has been mostly limited to manipulation tasks [13]. Manufacturing processes are often designed to be not only safe but as efficient as possible, leaving human comfort as a secondary goal. This is aggravated by the non-optimal behaviour often observed in humans when complying with social conventions [4]. For these reasons concepts like operator comfort, naturalness of motion, and sociability are often disregarded in shop-floor design.

Comfort in human-to-human interactions can be severely influenced by distance, with the necessary personal space dependent on the relationship, intention, and culture, as predicted by the theory of proxemics [5]. Transferring this human-human proxemics to human-robot proxemics [16] is one way of improving navigation systems [11, 14]. Inspired by the proxemics theory, human comfort can be increased by defining areas around humans with appropriate cost functions or potential fields [3, 10]. This approach allows robots to operate in close proximity to humans even in confined spaces, which is especially relevant in shop floors where the very high square footage cost promotes a high occupancy rate.

Respecting personal zones is only part of the problem as objects also interfere with human comfort and interaction. For instance, if a given screen is being attended by a person, the space between both must be free of obstacles, even if the obstacles do not violate the person's personal space [2]. However, if no one is attending to the screen, then the *affordance space* does not constitute an *activity space* [8] and, so, the presence of occluding obstacles causes no problems. In manufacturing, shelves in warehouses and assembly stations need to be always accessible to operators and, hence, there is an operational cost associated to having robots traversing that space that should be translated into the mobile robot's navigation cost map. To account for both spatial affordances of assembly stations and personal spaces of operators, the proposed system relies on layered cost maps [10].

This paper proposes that operators found by the robot while traversing the environment should induce the overlay of a cost function on the layered cost map according to the proxemics theory, thus ensuring that the mobile robot does not violate the operators' personal space. In the proposed system, assembly stations without assigned operators are simply represented as an obstacle in the layered cost map. The extent of the station's influence in the cost map is expanded, according to a conservative application of the proxemics theory, when an operator is known to be present therein. This way the mobile robot tends to avoid more strongly the station if the latter is assigned to an operator. Location, layout, task, and operator assignments of stations are assumed to be available to the robot via the factory's manufacturing enterprise systems (MES).

2   Proposed Human-Aware System

The fundamental aspect of this work is the application of the proxemics theory to the specificity of collaborative assembly scenarios and the use of a multiple layered costmap for its implementation (see Fig. 1). The costmap integrates three 2D layers, the first representing cost induced by the activity spaces of each station, $A(i,j)$, the second the cost reflected by the obstacles detected by range sensors, $O(i,j)$, and the third the cost resulting from the presence of the operators according to the proxemics theory, $P(i,j)$, where (i,j) is the index of each cell of the gridmap. The three layers are combined into a single cost map, $C(i,j)$, with a simple weighted average (as detailed below).

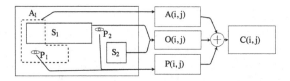

Fig. 1. System's layered cost map overview. The polygons with solid line and labelled S_1 and S_2 depict assembly stations while the polygon with the dotted line that is labelled A_1 depicts an activity space. Operators are represented by the objects with P_1 and P_2 labels. $A(i,j)$, $O(i,j)$, $P(i,j)$ are depictions of the costmap layers of activity spaces, obstacles, and operator presence, respectively. $C(i,j)$ is the fusion of all three layers, obtained with a simple weighted average.

The proposed navigation system adapts to the human presence and to the assembly environment with two simultaneous methods. The first method detects the operators inside the robot's sensors' field-of-view and associates to each of them a cost function based on the proxemics theory in a similar approach to the one proposed in [10]. Concretely, the layer contains each detected operator associated cost:

$$P(i,j) = \max\{P_1(i,j), ..., P_n(i,j)\}, \tag{1}$$
$$P_k(i,j) = \mathcal{N}_{x_k, y_k, \theta_k, \sigma_k}(i,j), \tag{2}$$

where n is the number of operators currently detected, and $P_k(i,j)$ represents the Gaussian-shaped cost induced by the personal space of operator k, and (x_k, y_k, θ_k) define the 2D pose of the operator and σ_k distribution's variance based on the personal space definition of the proxemics theory.

The second method maps the concept of *activity space* to every station of the shop-floor. Each activity space is spatially represented by its boundaries as a convex polygon. While each station can have multiple activity spaces, only one is considered at any given moment. Concretely, an activity space is only considered to the costmap if it is associated with current task's stage and if an operator has been detected inside its boundary (see Fig. 2(a)). The boundaries

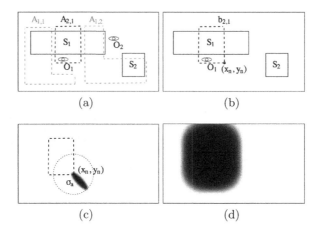

Fig. 2. Diagrams representing the work-flow of the creation of the multi-layered costmap activity layer. The polygons with solid line and labelled S_1 and S_2 depict assembly stations while the polygons with the dotted lines define activity spaces. (a) Activity space 2 of station 1 ($A_{2,1}$) activated by presence of operator O_1. (b) Convex polygon defined by boundary $b_{2,1}$ where each point (x_n, y_n) is iterated to create the final cost function. (c) To take into account the uncertainty of the operator's next position the ellipse of proxemic space is rotated 360° around each (x_n, y_n) point. (d) The final cost map of activity $A_{2,1}$.

of the station's activity spaces are extracted from the manufacturing enterprise system (MES) (see Fig. 2(b)). Each station s has at least one activity space a associated with its boundary, defined by $b_{a,s} = \{(x_1, y_1), ..., (x_n, y_n)\}$, where n is the number of points of the boundary's convex polygon. In the proxemics theory, personal space is represented as an directional anisotropic ellipse with the larger axis aligned with forward movement. However, the uncertainty associated with both the operator's detection and her/his next possible motion when in an assembly station needs to be addressed. To do so the directional anisotropic ellipse associated with personal space is fully rotated around each point of the activity space's boundary (see Fig. 2(c)).

The full revolution of the anisotropic ellipse is approximated by superposing a Gaussian function centred on each of the boundary points associated to a given activity space a of station s (see Fig. 2(c)):

$$A_{a,s}(i, j) = \max\{(\mathcal{N}_{x_m, y_m, \sigma_a}(i, j) : \forall (x_m, y_m) \in b_{a,s}\}, \tag{3}$$

where (x_m, y_m) represents a point along boundary $b_{a,s}$. Given that the robot's own tasks may require the navigation goal to be inside an activity space, represented by a_c, in that case it is not accounted for the activity layer:

$$A(i, j) = \max\{A_{a,s} : \forall a \in L_s \setminus \{a_c\}, s \in S\} \tag{4}$$

where L_s is the set of activity spaces for a given station s and S is the set of stations in the shopfloor. Both methods result in independent costmap layers that are fused with a layer with the obstacles detected by the robot's sensors and the map of the environment obtained via MES:

$$C(i,j) = \omega_o O(i,j) + \omega_p P(i,j) + \omega_a A(i,j), \tag{5}$$

where ω_o, ω_p, and ω_a are empirically defined weights associated with the obstacle layer, proxemics layer, and activity layers, respectively. The resulting costmap is then used to modulate the robot's navigation system behaviour.

3 Conclusions and Future Work

The proposed human-aware navigation system is being developed and tested both in simulation and in a real environment (see Fig. 3). The experimental setups created include multiple assembly stations, warehouses, and obstacles normally present in a shopfloor. Operators are also present performing real or simulated assembly tasks during the robot's operation. The robot model used in the experiments is the Intralogistics Mobile Assistant Unit (IMAU) developed for the intralogistics tasks in automotive shopfloor environments (for more detail refer to [9]). During these preliminary runs the system showed the ability to modulate navigation behaviour based on the detection of the operators and activity spaces (see Fig. 3).

(a)   (b)

Fig. 3. Snapshots of the preliminary experimental runs. (a) The simulation environment developed to mimic a automotive shopfloor. (b) The human operator being detected by the robot's onboard sensors during a preliminary run.

An human-aware navigation system for autonomous mobile robots capable of performing intralogistics tasks in assembly shopfloors was presented. A set of preliminary experiments in both simulation and lab environment showed the potential of the proposed system to affect the navigation of the mobile robot to increase operator comfort. Based on a multi-layered costmap the proposed system models both activity spaces and operators in different layers and fuses them with obstacle information. Exploiting offline information of task type, topology, and online detection of operators, the system reduces the number of violations of the operators personal space. In the future we expect to validate the system in a larger variety of environments and applications inside the manufacturing scope. Finally, we also intend to improve the system by learning operator's behaviour in each specific task introducing this information into a novel estimator. We also aim to improve the cost representation of the different stations and tasks by gathering information from all sensors present in the shopfloor, reducing temporal uncertainty related to each operator's location.

References

1. Bogh, S., Schou, C., Rühr, T., Kogan, Y., Dömel, A., Brucker, M., Eberst, C., Tornese, R., Sprunk, C., Tipaldi, G.D., et al.: Integration and assessment of multiple mobile manipulators in a real-world industrial production facility. In: Proceedings of 41st International Symposium on Robotics ISR/Robotik 2014, pp. 1–8. VDE (2014)
2. Bransford, J., Shaw, R.E.: Perceiving, Acting, and Knowing: Toward an Ecological Psychology. Lawrence Erlbaum Associates, New York (1977). Distribuited by the Halsted Press dision of John Wiley and sons
3. Chik, S.F., Yeong, C.F., Su, E.L.M., Lim, T.Y., Duan, F., Tan, J.T.C., Tan, P.H., Chin, P.J.H.: Gaussian pedestrian proxemics model with social force for service robot navigation in dynamic environment. In: Mohamed Ali, M.S., Wahid, H., Mohd Subha, N.A., Sahlan, S., Md. Yunus, M.A., Wahap, A.R. (eds.) AsiaSim 2017. CCIS, vol. 751, pp. 61–73. Springer, Singapore (2017). https://doi.org/10.1007/978-981-10-6463-0_6
4. Chung, S.Y., Huang, H.P.: Incremental learning of human social behaviors with feature-based spatial effects. In: International Conference on Intelligent Robots and Systems (IROS), pp. 2417–2422. IEEE (2012)
5. Hall, E.: The Hidden Dimension: Man's Use of Space in Public and in Private. Bodley Head, London (1969)
6. Hvilshøj, M., Bøgh, S.: "Little Helper" – an autonomous industrial mobile manipulator concept. Int. J. Adv. Robot. Syst. **8**(2), 15 (2011)
7. Kruse, T., Pandey, A.K., Alami, R., Kirsch, A.: Human-aware robot navigation: a survey. Robot. Auton. Syst. **61**(12), 1726–1743 (2013)
8. Lindner, F., Eschenbach, C.: Towards a formalization of social spaces for socially aware robots. In: Egenhofer, M., Giudice, N., Moratz, R., Worboys, M. (eds.) COSIT 2011. LNCS, vol. 6899, pp. 283–303. Springer, Heidelberg (2011). https://doi.org/10.1007/978-3-642-23196-4_16
9. Lourenço, A., Marques, F., Mendonça, R., Pinto, E., Barata, J.: On the design of the ROBO–PARTNER intra-factory logistics autonomous robot. In: 2016 IEEE International Conference on Systems, Man, and Cybernetics (SMC), pp. 2647–2652. IEEE (2016)
10. Lu, D.V., Hershberger, D., Smart, W.D.: Layered costmaps for context-sensitive navigation. In: 2014 IEEE/RSJ International Conference on Intelligent Robots and Systems (IROS 2014), pp. 709–715. IEEE (2014)
11. Luber, M., Spinello, L., Silva, J., Arras, K.O.: Socially-aware robot navigation: a learning approach. In: 2012 IEEE/RSJ International Conference on Intelligent Robots and Systems (IROS), pp. 902–907. IEEE (2012)
12. Matthias, B., Kock, S., Jerregard, H., Källman, M., Lundberg, I.: Safety of collaborative industrial robots: certification possibilities for a collaborative assembly robot concept. In: IEEE International Symposium on Assembly and Manufacturing (ISAM 2011), pp. 1–6. IEEE (2011)

13. Michalos, G., Makris, S., Tsarouchi, P., Guasch, T., Kontovrakis, D., Chryssolouris, G.: Design considerations for safe human-robot collaborative workplaces. Procedia CIrP **37**, 248–253 (2015)
14. Rios-Martinez, J., Spalanzani, A., Laugier, C.: From proxemics theory to socially-aware navigation: a survey. Int. J. Soc. Robot. **7**(2), 137–153 (2015)
15. Sprunk, C., Lau, B., Pfaff, P., Burgard, W.: An accurate and efficient navigation system for omnidirectional robots in industrial environments. Auton. Robots **41**(2), 473–493 (2017)
16. Takayama, L., Pantofaru, C.: Influences on proxemic behaviors in human-robot interaction. In: IEEE/RSJ International Conference on Intelligent Robots and Systems, IROS, pp. 5495–5502. IEEE (2009)

Towards the Simplicity of Complex Interfaces: Applying Ephemeral Adaptation to Enhance User Performance and Satisfaction

Peter A. M. Ruijten[(✉)], Evine Kruyt-Beursken, and Wijnand A. IJsselsteijn

Eindhoven University of Technology, Eindhoven, The Netherlands
`p.a.m.ruijten@tue.nl`

Abstract. In interface design of complex information systems, there is a well-known trade-off between transparently communicating all possible user actions, and not creating information overload by only communicating those actions that are relevant for a specific user at a specific point. Differences in user expertise can provide further challenges to interaction design, as no one-size-fits-all solution accommodates all user types. A solution to this is ephemeral adaptation, a symbiotic system in which attention is steered towards relevant items by making them appear immediately, while other items fade in over time. To date, this concept has only been tested in a simple set-up with drop-down menu's, where the usability outcome measures were measured immediately after initial exposure to the interface. Ephemeral adaptation was applied within complex software, allowing an exploration of its potential value and evaluations on usability over time. Results showed increased performance of novice users, showing potential benefits of ephemeral adaptation.

Keywords: Ephemeral adaptation · Interface design
Symbiotic system · Blueriq

1 Introduction

"The story of usability is a perverse journey from simplicity to complexity. That's right, from simplicity to complexity — not the other way around."

Mads Soegaard, 2012.

The reasoning behind Soegaard's point of view is the notion that, despite over 35 years of progress in usability research, interactions with technology can still be baffling and frustrating. With the proliferation of wearable and mobile technologies, the interconnectedness of devices (IoT), and the augmentation or virtualisation of nearly every human activity, we see a new level of diversity and ubiquity of user interfaces that challenges interaction designers. At the same

J. Ham et al. (Eds.): Symbiotic 2017, LNCS 10727, pp. 86–97, 2018.
https://doi.org/10.1007/978-3-319-91593-7_10

time, we are still struggling with some of the 'classic' interaction design challenges surrounding complex professional information and control systems, such as complex process control software, ERP software, or financial support systems. Here, more than anything, the problem of information overload is salient, and solutions are sought in adaptive interfaces that present context- and task-relevant information only, that is, ideally, tailored to the level of expertise of the individual user.

This sets many new challenges for designers who aim to detect user preferences and goals and develop interfaces in such a way that they adapt to those preferences. One way of adapting an interface to its user is to first present the most relevant items, and only after that linearly fade in other items. This form of interface design is called ephemeral adaptation [5].

In this paper, we investigate whether adding ephemeral adaptation to an interface increases performance of novice users of a complex software program. We first outline the importance of personalizing interfaces and discuss different types of users and their experiences with complex interfaces. Next, we briefly introduce the software to be used in the study, after which we present a user study on the effects of ephemeral adaptation. We end with a discussion on potential opportunities and downsides of ephemeral adaptation in complex interfaces.

1.1   Personalizing Interfaces

Personalized interactions are becoming commonplace in domains such as persuasive technology [11,12], human-robot interaction [13], and graphical user interfaces [4]. What these have in common is the argument that a strategy that works for one type of user may not have the same effect on another. Adapting interfaces to their users could increase positive evaluations of advertisements [10], (healthy) behavior [15], and efficiency [4].

Findlater and McGrenere [4] distinguish four aspects that are important for personalized interfaces: control, granularity, visibility of change and frequency of change. With control they refer to the extent to which the user is in control of the adaptation. Granularity means that the ability to customize an interface ranges between general (in which users can only modify the interface on a higher level) and specific (in which a user can modify each feature). Visibility of change can be implemented by reorganizing items by moving, hiding, re-sizing, or replicating them in order to reduce navigation time. Frequency of change refers to a time aspect, which is especially interesting for adaptive approaches because it appears to affect both costs and benefits of user interfaces [6].

Benefits of personalizing interfaces are that it can fulfill specific user needs [7], thereby strongly increasing user satisfaction. Personalizing interfaces could however also have adverse affects; it could negatively impact users' awareness of the full set of available features [4]. Allowing users to discover new features of an interface is an important factor that helps overcoming such a lack in feature-awareness, and should be taken into consideration when designing interfaces. Another negative effect of personalizing interfaces is a potential performance dip that occurs when users switch to a new, more advanced, interface [2].

So, despite the potential benefits of personalizing interfaces, it may also negatively influence people's ability to learn using the software in the most optimal way.

1.2   Differences in User Expertise

People's ability to learn new aspects of interfaces depends on their expertise with the system. Shneiderman [17] and Wickens [18] assign different values to two types of users: novices and experts. Novice users tend to use open-ended strategies when discovering how interfaces work [17], and prefer feed-forward as well as informative feedback to confirm actions. They may not be familiar with an interface's terminology and rely more on visual cues. Chunks of items are those that are semantically related, but the ability to chunk information depends on expertise, thus only small chunks should be used for novice users [18]. Novice users also thrive when the cognitive demands of an interface are relatively low, for example when there is a low need for divided attention [18].

Experts rely more on densely packed displays and a fast pace of interaction. They are more comfortable with different types of feedback, as long as it does not distract from the task at hand [17]. They also need to work efficiently, and accomplish this by using short-cuts and keys instead of the mouse [18].

One clear difference between the needs of these two types of users is in the visual display of information. While expert users prefer a densely packed display with many options to select from, novice users are better off with a less cluttered view of the available options. Matching the design of an interface to these needs could increase the learnability of a complex interface. Grossman et al. [9] defined two stages of learnability: initial learnability, covering the initial performance with the system, and extended learnability, covering the change in performance over time. We refer to extended learnability as memorability; the extent to which you can still use an interface *after* you have learned how to use it.

1.3   Ephemeral Adaptation

Any progress in software performance starts with the awareness of what the software has to offer. Cockburn et al. [2] reviewed interface elements supporting software learnability in order to help users transition to the level of an expert user. One of those elements is ephemeral adaptation. With ephemeral adaptation, attention is drawn to items in a menu that are most applicable to the user. This is done by manipulating the time of appearance of items, such that items predicted to be most interesting to the user are shown immediately, while the other items linearly fade in over 500 ms. Findlater et al. [5] showed that a pull-down menu with ephemeral adaptation was more effective and satisfying compared to a normal pull-down menu in which all items are shown immediately or a highlighted menu in which important components were highlighted.

Ephemeral interfaces utilize spatial attention processes, by first presenting a limited set of items relevant to a task, and next, showing the full gamut of interface options. Using spatial memory, users are expected to be able to remember the relevant items in the context of the larger, more complicated interface. Due to the potential value of this technique and its applicability in complex software design, the current study will focus on ephemeral adaptation utilizing a realistic interface of a complex end-user programming system - the Blueriq programming environment, described in Sect. 2.

1.4   Research Aims

In order to test the potential benefits of adding ephemeral adaptation to a complex interface, an existing program was used and adapted to include ephemeral adaptation. This software was used in a study that investigated effects of ephemeral adaptation on user performance, measured through efficiency (i.e. how fast tasks are performed) and effectiveness (i.e. how well tasks are performed). Ephemeral adaptation was expected to increase user performance. In addition, user experiences were collected to provide more qualitative insights into people's subjective evaluations of ephemeral adaptation.

2   Blueriq Software

The interface that was used for the study is Blueriq Studio [1], which supports the creation of applications for the government, banks and insurance companies and services [3]. Most of those applications consist of a number of front-end pages that are visible for the users, and a back-end in which data is stored and connections are made. The complexity of the interface is shown in Fig. 1.

Fig. 1. Visualization of the interface consisting of five components, indicated as (A) the ribbon, (B) the left bar, (C) the list with instances of a particular type, (D) the canvas, and (E) the project.

Several concepts are needed for creating an application: entities (components such as 'room', 'person', and 'reservation'), attributes (such as 'name' and 'date of birth' for persons), containers (groups of information that belongs together, such as attributes, buttons, and text), pages (which are the pages in the front-end part of the application), and value-lists (which are essentially labels for attributes). When novice users are confronted with the interface for the first time, they tend to apply inefficient trial and error strategies.

3 Methods

3.1 Participants and Design

Forty eight students (21 males and 27 females; age $M = 21.0$, $SD = 2.1$, Range $= 18$ to 26) were randomly assigned to one of two Interface types: a normal interface ($n = 23$) or an interface with ephemeral adaptation ($n = 25$). Of those 48 participants, 25 (11 males and 14 females; age $M = 21.4$, $SD = 2.3$, Range $= 18$ to 26) completed the experiment and attended a second session. None of the participants had any experience with the software used in the study. The experiment consisted of two lab-sessions and an in-between learning phase of 5 days, see Fig. 2. The dependent variables were performance (efficiency and effectiveness) and feature awareness.

3.2 Materials

Most participants performed the study on their own laptop[1], and those who did not own a laptop used a desktop computer with a 22" LCD flat-screen. Participants could access the Blueriq software in their browser after adjusting some security settings. Readability of the labels was tested on screens with varying sizes, and found to be similar in all cases. For half the participants, the interface of the program was manipulated to include ephemeral adaptation in the biggest part of the interface (the canvas; component D in Fig. 1). The application of ephemeral adaptation resulted in immediate visibility of the most important fields, and a 2.5 s fade-in of all other fields together. This 2.5 s fade-in time was chosen based on a pilot study.

Three assignments were developed; creating a hotel reservation system, building an application to apply for a job, and designing an interface for creating a bank account. In each of these assignments, a set of tasks was created that tapped into all of the concepts (i.e. entities 3x, attributes 7x, containers 2x, pages 2x, and value-lists 1x). The number of tasks was chosen such that no large difference between completion times were expected. To help novice users understand the differences between the concepts, two instruction videos were created in which the basics of using the interface were explained.

---

[1] With a 15.6" screen.

3.3   Measures

Performance was measured on effectiveness and efficiency. Effectiveness refers to the number of tasks people completed and the last task they completed. The latter was included because some tasks could be skipped in the assignments. Efficiency refers to the time needed to complete the tasks. Feature awareness was measured with a recognition questionnaire, in which people indicated whether or not items existed in the software interface. The questionnaire consisted of twelve existing and six distraction items. Feature awareness was the percentage of correct answers on the questionnaire, ranging from 0 to 1.

Participants who attended the second session evaluated the software through several open questions that provided more qualitative data on people's evaluations of a system that applies ephemeral adaptation.

3.4   Procedure

Upon arrival at the lab, participants read an informed consent form that explained their rights as participant. After signing the form, participants watched the first of the two instruction videos. They could follow the guidelines in the video to open the software in their browser. Next, they were presented with the first assignment (creating a hotel reservation system) that contained a step-by-step guide on how to build an application to book a hotel room. After a number of steps, participants were instructed to start the second instruction video while continuing with the assignment. After 20 min, participants were automatically logged out, and they completed the recognition questionnaire. The first session lasted for 40 min, and participants who did not continue with the second phase were debriefed and received a compensation of €7.

Those who did continue worked on the second assignment from home for five consecutive days, ten minutes per day. In order to prevent errors, the starting point of each practice day was set up in advance. After five days, participants returned to the lab for session 2. During this session, participants worked on the third assignment (designing an interface for creating a bank account). There were no instruction videos, and all participants worked in the software interface without ephemeral adaptation. After 20 min, participants were automatically logged out and completed the recognition questionnaire and the open questions that measured their evaluations of the software. Participation in the whole experiment took about 2 h in total, for which participants were compensated with €18. At the end of the session, participants were debriefed, paid, and thanked for their contribution. A time-line of the experiment is shown in Fig. 2.

4   Results

Due to a number of technical issues with the software, several people were not able to complete specific tasks or assignments. For this reason, sample sizes are reported for each condition in all analyses. In order to fairly compare performance between the two interface types, we decided to keep exposure time with

Session 1					Learning phase					Session 2			
Day 1					Day 2	Day 3	Day 4	Day 5	Day 6	Day 7			
Instructions	Video 1	Start Blueriq	Assignment 1 & Video 2	Questionnaire	Assignment 2 Part 1	Assignment 2 Part 2	Assignment 2 Part 3	Assignment 2 Part 4	Assignment 2 Part 5	Assignment 3	Questionnaire	Open questions	Payment
5m	5m	8m	20m	2m	10m	10m	10m	10m	10m	20m	2m	6m	2m
40m					50m					30m			

Fig. 2. Visualization of the time-line of the experiment.

the software equal for all participants. For this reason, data were cut-off at the time in which the fastest participant completed all tasks: 18 min and 22 s in session 1 and 11 min and 4 s in session 2.

4.1 Effectiveness

To test the effect of Interface type on effectiveness, the number of completed tasks and the last completed task in both sessions were submitted to independent samples t-tests with the two Interface types as groups. Results showed a marginally significant effect for the number of tasks finished in session 1 (with $t(35) = 1.83$, $p = 0.075$, $d = 0.60$). More specifically, the number of completed tasks in session 1 was higher for the ephemeral interface ($n = 19$, $M = 9.53$, $SD = 3.44$) than the normal interface ($n = 18$, $M = 7.44$, $SD = 3.47$), see Fig. 3a. No significant effects of Interface type were found on any of the other variables (all t's < 1, all p's > 0.65).

4.2 Efficiency

To test the effect of Interface type on efficiency, the average completion time for each type of task (entities, attributes, containers, pages, and value-lists) in both sessions were submitted to independent samples t-tests with the two Interface types as groups. Results showed significant effects for the average completion time of entities (with $t(45) = 2.01$, $p = 0.050$, $d = 0.58$) and attributes (with $t(45) = 2.21$, $p = 0.033$, $d = 0.66$) in session 1. More specifically, the completion time for entities (in ms) in session 1 was lower for the ephemeral interface ($n = 24$, $M = 39$, $SD = 80.7$) than the normal interface ($n = 23$, $M = 154$, $SD = 268.4$). Likewise, the completion time for attributes in session 1 was lower for the ephemeral interface ($n = 24$, $M = 112$, $SD = 129.2$) than the normal interface ($n = 20$, $M = 227$, $SD = 209.9$). These results are visualized in Fig. 3b. No significant effects of Interface type were found on any of the other variables (all t's < 1.2, all p's > 0.27).

4.3 Feature Awareness

To test the effect of Interface type on Feature awareness, average recognition percentages in both sessions were submitted to independent samples t-tests with

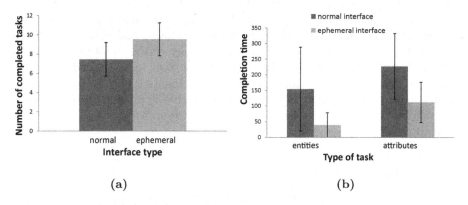

Fig. 3. Visualization of effects on performance measures, with (a) number of completed tasks, and (b) average completion times for entities (in ms) for the two experimental conditions. Whiskers represent standard deviations.

the two Interface types as groups. Results showed no significant effect of Interface type in either of the sessions (both t's < 1, both p's > 0.35).

4.4   User Evaluations

Most participants were positive about the interface. Some indicated that they needed some time to get adjusted to it, but after a while they got more used to it. One participant in the ephemeral interface condition stated that *'at first it was a lot of information, but after working with the software more often, the amount of information was fine and clear'*, and one in the normal interface condition stated that *'all necessary options were visible on the screen right away'*.

It appeared that participants in the normal interface condition seemed to complain more about the amount of information than those in the ephemeral interface condition. Those in the normal interface condition stated that there was *'much more information than I needed'*, or that there was *'quite some information-overload the first few times I used the software'*, and *'there were many buttons of which I did not know what to do with them'*, while participants in the ephemeral interface condition complained more about *'high [complexity] for a simple program'*, or that *'some of the options were not or hardly explained'*.

This difference was confirmed by the answers participants gave to the question what they would like to change in the interface. Participants in the normal interface condition stated they would like to have *'much fewer buttons and screens'* and preferred the software to *'show fewer buttons and options on the starting screen'*. Despite the notion that some participants in the ephemeral interface condition also stated that they wanted a menu that is *'simpler, maybe in Dutch'*, the majority of answers focused on very different aspects such as clearer icons, color themes, and *'fancy design'*.

When asked what they liked about the interface, some participants in the ephemeral interface condition pointed out that *'the interface was very supportive at the start'* and that they *'did not need to search that long to find a function'.* Participants in the normal interface condition were also positive, but related this more to the *'business-like presentation'* and *'proper clustering of items'.*

Finally, when asked whether they noticed that some items needed more time to become fully visible, only four out of 13 participants in the ephemeral adaptation condition stated that they did, indicating that applying ephemeral adaptation did not make them aware of being guided towards a specific functionality of the interface.

5   Discussion

The current work addressed the issue of information overload in complex interfaces that support tasks which require a significant learning curve for novice users. One potential improvement of the user interface is the use of ephemeral adaptation [5]. In ephemeral adaptation, the most relevant information is shown before the full complexity is revealed. The use of ephemeral adaptation may reduce clutter and guide novice users to the most important items or options, thereby reducing the initial effort needed to familiarize with more complex software. Previous research has shown positive effects of ephemeral adaptation in a simple interface [5], but effects within more complicated software environments were largely unknown.

The potential benefits for novice users of adding ephemeral adaptation to a complex interface were tested in a study that measured user performance and evaluations of an existing program. There was a trend showing that novice users tended to complete more tasks and need less time to finish certain tasks when provided with an interface that applies ephemeral adaptation. In addition, users of the software with ephemeral adaptation mentioned fewer problems with information overload. Due to a low number of participants and the notion that this effect was not significant, it is hard to draw solid conclusions from this.

Interestingly, the effects of ephemeral adaptation on performance were only found in the first session, indicating that it only improved performance during the first use of the software. It should be noted that all participants made use of the interface without ephemeral adaptation in the second session, where no differences in performance were found. Thus, getting used to the ephemeral interface did not have any negative effects on people's performance with the normal interface, which shows potential benefits of ephemeral adaptation during first time usage, but also highlight the fact that these benefits may be less prominent after long-term use of an interface.

The efficiency of finishing tasks was higher when ephemeral adaptation was applied. That is, people needed less time to complete tasks involving entities and attributes, whereas no differences were found on tasks involving containers, pages, and value-lists. These latter types of tasks mostly involved the construction of pages and connecting pieces of information to each other, while tasks involving entities and attributes all included the creation of something new. It should not come as a surprise that ephemeral adaptation was beneficial for these types of tasks specifically, because it is those types of tasks that benefit most from visual guidance.

5.1 Limitations and Future Work

Participants were given access to an online environment that could track their performance with the software. Due to technical problems, some of them could not finish any of the tasks. Because of this, many participants were only able to participate in the first session of the experiment, reducing the sample size in the second session by almost 50%. This small sample size made us decide to include the qualitative questions at the end of the second session, giving us valuable insights in people's experiences with the software.

Ephemeral adaptation was only applied to one aspect of the interface (the Canvas), while some of the tasks made use of different areas as well. This could have been a reason for finding no or only marginally significant effects of Interface type. Future studies should apply ephemeral adaptation to multiple areas of an interface and test whether its positive effects on people's performance could be enhanced.

Some of the participants were relatively fast in finishing all the tasks of the assignments. In order to have a fair comparison, we decided to create a cut-off point and have all participants have the same exposure time with the software. This cut-off point would not have been necessary if we created more tasks than people could finish in the time they were given. In addition, some people practiced for less than 10 min every day, while others did make use of the full practice time, causing a difference in exposure time before the start of session 2. These differences were not found to be correlated to any of the performance measures, but care should be given to making sure that exposure time is constant between participants in further studies.

The experiment only involved novice users, making it impossible to make any general claims about different types of (more advanced) users. However, we believe that ephemeral adaptation is especially helpful for inexperienced users while not being harmful for more experienced ones. Nevertheless, there is an important differentiation between a user interface and the content of a task [8], and ephemeral adaptation is only beneficial for gaining expertise on low-level dimensions of the user interface.

Ephemeral adaptation is just one method for assisting novice users in becoming experts. Other methods include menus that apply directional movements for selecting items [2], promoting command line use to less experienced users [16], and so-called skillometers that help users reflect on software expertise and learnability [14]. While all these methods have been shown to have potentially beneficial effects, ephemeral adaptation could easily be adapted to individual users by taking their previous actions in the interface into account.

5.2 Conclusions

Ephemeral adaptation appears to be beneficial for novice users in a complex interface, and it could help facilitating a smooth transition to a normal interface. It reduces information overload by adding a temporal dimension to interface design, thereby keeping the interface consistent in its appearance and functionality.

The next step is to make ephemeral adaptation adaptable to individual user behavior. It should learn from its users and present a complex interface in such a way that users are easily guided towards the functions that they are most likely needing at any moment. The immediate visibility of only those important items reduces complexity and can be applied in multiple complex software programs. As such, diminishing the initial effort needed to understand a complex interface may ultimately result in better user experiences, and flips the story of usability to one from complexity to simplicity.

References

1. Blueriq: Make your own rules (2017). https://www.blueriq.com/en/. Accessed 10 June 2017
2. Cockburn, A., Gutwin, C., Scarr, J., Malacria, S.: Supporting novice to expert transitions in user interfaces. ACM Comput. Surv. (CSUR) **47**(2), 31 (2015)
3. Everest: Business engineering (2017). https://www.everest.nl/. Accessed 10 June 2017
4. Findlater, L., McGrenere, J.: Beyond performance: feature awareness in personalized interfaces. Int. J. Hum Comput Stud. **68**(3), 121–137 (2010)
5. Findlater, L., Moffatt, K., McGrenere, J., Dawson, J.: Ephemeral adaptation: the use of gradual onset to improve menu selection performance. In: Proceedings of the SIGCHI Conference on Human Factors in Computing Systems, pp. 1655–1664. ACM (2009)
6. Gajos, K.Z., Czerwinski, M., Tan, D.S., Weld, D.S.: Exploring the design space for adaptive graphical user interfaces. In: Proceedings of the Working Conference on Advanced Visual Interfaces, pp. 201–208. ACM (2006)
7. Gajos, K.Z., Everitt, K., Tan, D.S., Czerwinski, M., Weld, D.S.: Predictability and accuracy in adaptive user interfaces. In: Proceedings of the SIGCHI Conference on Human Factors in Computing Systems, pp. 1271–1274. ACM (2008)
8. Grossman, T., Fitzmaurice, G.: An investigation of metrics for the in situ detection of software expertise. Hum.-Comput. Interact. **30**(1), 64–102 (2015)
9. Grossman, T., Fitzmaurice, G., Attar, R.: A survey of software learnability: metrics, methodologies and guidelines. In: Proceedings of the SIGCHI Conference on Human Factors in Computing Systems, pp. 649–658. ACM (2009)
10. Hirsh, J.B., Kang, S.K., Bodenhausen, G.V.: Personalized persuasion tailoring persuasive appeals to recipients personality traits. Psychol. Sci. **23**(6), 578–581 (2012)
11. Kaptein, M., Lacroix, J., Saini, P.: Individual differences in persuadability in the health promotion domain. In: Ploug, T., Hasle, P., Oinas-Kukkonen, H. (eds.) PERSUASIVE 2010. LNCS, vol. 6137, pp. 94–105. Springer, Heidelberg (2010). https://doi.org/10.1007/978-3-642-13226-1_11

12. Kaptein, M., Markopoulos, P., de Ruyter, B., Aarts, E.: Can you be persuaded? individual differences in susceptibility to persuasion. In: Gross, T., Gulliksen, J., Kotzé, P., Oestreicher, L., Palanque, P., Prates, R.O., Winckler, M. (eds.) INTER-ACT 2009. LNCS, vol. 5726, pp. 115–118. Springer, Heidelberg (2009). https://doi.org/10.1007/978-3-642-03655-2_13

13. Lee, M.K., Forlizzi, J., Kiesler, S., Rybski, P., Antanitis, J., Savetsila, S.: Personalization in HRI: a longitudinal field experiment. In: 2012 7th ACM/IEEE International Conference on Human-Robot Interaction (HRI), pp. 319–326. IEEE (2012)

14. Malacria, S., Scarr, J., Cockburn, A., Gutwin, C., Grossman, T.: Skillometers: reflective widgets that motivate and help users to improve performance. In: Proceedings of the 26th Annual ACM Symposium on User Interface Software and Technology, pp. 321–330. ACM (2013)

15. Sakai, R., Van Peteghem, S., van de Sande, L., Banach, P., Kaptein, M.: Personalized persuasion in ambient intelligence: the apstairs system. In: Keyson, D.V., Maher, M.L., Streitz, N., Cheok, A., Augusto, J.C., Wichert, R., Englebienne, G., Aghajan, H., Kröse, B.J.A. (eds.) AmI 2011. LNCS, vol. 7040, pp. 205–209. Springer, Heidelberg (2011). https://doi.org/10.1007/978-3-642-25167-2_26

16. Scarr, J., Cockburn, A., Gutwin, C., Quinn, P.: Dips and ceilings: understanding and supporting transitions to expertise in user interfaces. In: Proceedings of the Sigchi Conference on Human Factors in Computing Systems, pp. 2741–2750. ACM (2011)

17. Shneiderman, B., Plaisant, C., Cohen, M.S., Jacobs, S., Elmqvist, N., Diakopoulos, N.: Designing the User Interface: Strategies for Effective Human-computer Interaction. Pearson (2016)

18. Wickens, C.D., Hollands, J.G., Banbury, S., Parasuraman, R.: Engineering Psychology & Human Performance. Psychology Press (2015)

Persuasive Virtual Touch: The Effect of Artificial Social Touch on Shopping Behavior in Virtual Reality

Yuguang Zhao[1], Jaap Ham[1(✉)], and Jurgen van der Vlist[2]

[1] Eindhoven University of Technology, Human-Technology Interaction,
PO Box 513, 5600 MB Eindhoven, The Netherlands
j.r.c.ham@tue.nl
[2] Enversed B.V., Torenallee 100-02, 5617 BE Eindhoven, The Netherlands

Abstract. Virtual reality (VR) technology affords powerful influences on human behavior and thinking through symbiotic interaction between the VR environment and the human user. Earlier research indicated that in a real bookstore, a slight touch by the welcoming shop assistant on the shopper's upper arm positively influenced consumer behavior. To investigate effects of artificial social touch in VR, participants were asked to shop in two virtual shops (in random order). The virtual shop assistant touched participants (shoppers) on the upper arm (through an actuator on participant's arm) while greeting, or, in the other shop, identically greeted participants without touching them. Results showed that in the shop in which participants were touched by the virtual shop assistant, they spent more time, more money on purchasing and their overall shopping experience evaluation was more positive. Findings confirmed that the illusion of virtual social touch can be established in VR and contributed that VR employing artificial social touch can be effective in influencing consumer behavior.

Keywords: Virtual reality · Persuasive technology · Persuasive VR
Shopping behavior · Interpersonal touch

1 Introduction

Imagine that one day in the near future you are shopping in a Virtual Reality (VR) shop. The virtual shop assistant greets you, and touches you on the upper arm while doing so. You can not only see the virtual assistant but also feel the touch in VR. Would that touch influence your shopping behavior and make you buy more?

Indeed, VR is no longer a new concept in modern society. VR is a computer technology that is often regarded as a natural extension of 3D computer graphics with advanced input and output devices. Sometimes VR is combined with physical spaces or multi-projected environments, to generate realistic images, sounds and other sensations, which give users a sense of reality [10]. Several companies have released their VR equipment on the consumer market, like for instance the Oculus Rift consumer version [18], SONY PlayStation VR [19] and HTC Vive [26]. VR technology has been used in many domains, not only entertainment, but also for serious purposes, such as skills training [25], influencing egress behavior [4] and clinical therapies [11].

Another emerging (commercial) use of VR is VR shopping. In traditional online shopping, consumers can only see products pictures on screen. VR technology can boost their shopping experience into a new level. With simply a VR headset, consumers can view the item from every angle, as if the product was in front of them. Also, VR shopping can outperform traditional real-world shopping in several aspects. For example, the virtual environment is much more flexible than physical space. It is easier to evaluate and redesign shopping environments (e.g., shops) without high cost. Also, it reduces the possibility of returns which may cost a lot.

In traditional retail environments, scientific theories help retailers understand human motivation for shopping behavior. One of the important theories is the PAD emotional state model proposed by Mehrabian and Russell (1974). PAD stands for pleasure, arousal and dominance [15]. The model indicates that any environment, including that of a retail store, will produce an emotional state in an individual that can be characterized in terms of the three PAD dimensions, which are factorially orthogonal. Earlier research suggested that pleasure and arousal are significant mediators of shopping behaviors within the store [21]. That is, [21] found in their experiment that pleasure is a very powerful determinant of consumer behaviors within the store, including spending behavior, and that arousal can increase time spent in the store and also willingness to interact with sales personnel [21]. The third emotional state, dominance, however, was not very relevant to instore behavior [21].

Related to the consumer's emotional state, human sales agents are also a factor that will influence the shopper's behavior in traditional retail environment. Human sales agents are very important for increasing satisfaction with a retailer, enhance attitudes toward products sold by the retailer and increase the consumer's intention to buy [27].

In an online shopping environment (e.g., a web shop), however, there is no direct communication between consumer and shop assistant. To deal with the problem of no direct communication between consumer and shop assistant, an artificial social agent can be used as persuasion agent [22]. Thereby, interactions within such (online, but also VR) environments become more like symbiotic interactions [31].

Artificial social agents can be used to influence people's behavior or attitudes, just as human agents do in many situations [22]. People tend to react to computer technology as though it was a real social entity, according to the media equation hypothesis [20]. This tendency to treat computer technology as a social entity occurs independent of whether the representation of the computer is the screen, a voice, or an agent [17]. Relatedly, Social Agency Theory [13] and the Social Cue Hypothesis [12] suggested that the more social cues (e.g., voice, presence of a face, face expressions) technological systems display, the more social the interaction between a human and the technology becomes [22].

Confirming this, Holzwarth and colleagues (2006) showed that using a virtual sales agent in an online shop led to more satisfaction with the retailer, a more positive attitude toward the product, and a greater purchase intention [8], suggesting that artificial sales agents in online environments have abilities similar to those of a real shop assistant [8].

Another very interesting variable that can influence the shopper's behavior is interpersonal touch: whether the shopper is touched by shop assistant in the social context of shopping. In general, earlier research suggested that interpersonal touch can facilitate perceptions of liking and trustworthiness [9]. For example, Mehrabian (1971) found that body contact is a signal of liking and acceptance [14]. More specifically, interpersonal touch can also have an influence on consumers' feelings and judgements, as shown for example by Wycoff and Holley (1990), who reported that those passengers touched by an airline flight attendant on the shoulder or forearm increased their liking of the flight attendant and the airline in general, and reported increased safety perceptions [28]. For an overview on social touch, see Gallace and Spence (2008; [29]), and for an overview on mediated social touch, see Haans and IJsselsteijn [30].

Showing that social touch can influence consumer shopping behavior, Hornik (1991) conducted an experiment in a book store. When shoppers entered the store, they were first greeted by an experimenter. Half of the shoppers were touched by the experimenter on the upper arm while the other half was not. Results indicated that participants who were touched by the experimenters spent more time and more money in the store, and also evaluated the store more positively [9]. Interestingly, although [9] found effects of touch for both genders, [9] also found that the effects of touch were moderated by gender of the participant.

Indeed, touch is one of the most primitive means of contact and communication [9]. Different types of touch have different meanings. For instance, handshake is one of the most common body signals which can be interpreted as polite and friendly [9]. Holding the upper arm while shaking hands is influencing and persuading form of touch [5].

Also in VR, haptic feedback can be used to provide the feeling of being touched by another (virtual) person, making the interaction more symbiotic (see [31]). Haptic feedback can be considered a crucial sensorial modality in virtual reality interactions [3]. Haptics means both force feedback (simulating object hardness, weight, and inertia) and tactile feedback (simulating surface contact geometry, smoothness, slippage, and temperature) [3]. In the current research, we focus on tactile feedback, more specifically, simulating surface contact. Earlier research indicated that tactile feedback can enhance the realism of virtual environments [7].

Based on the theories presented above, we argue that social touch can influence consumer shopping behavior also in VR. More specifically, based on the Media Equation hypothesis [20] we argue that users' responses to the social cues that artificial social agents in VR display will be comparable to their responses to social cues by humans. Therefore, just like the human shop assistant in [9], artificial social agents using artificial social touch in VR also have persuasive power and can help to increase sales. Interpersonal touch also has persuasive power and helps increase sales.

VR is a powerful simulation tool, it can provide vivid and immersive experience, which may have advantage for persuasive purposes and influencing behavior, and have positive influences on consumer's purchasing behavior. However, research of VR as a persuasive technology is relatively rare. Previous studies of persuasion in VR mainly focused on influencing people in general. To our knowledge, earlier research has not investigated the persuasive effects of interpersonal touch in VR. VR has potential persuasive power and VR shopping can be a huge promising market in near future. Therefore, it is important to investigate whether artificial social touch can be effective in VR.

Importantly, extending research of persuasion in real life contexts, studying this question in VR allows for very precise identification of the social cues that are effective. That is, the research on the effectiveness of social touch in a real shop [9] leaves open the possibility that in addition to touching, the sales agent used also other social cues in the touch condition (e.g., small smiles or eye movements). VR technology allows to control all characteristics and behavior of the artificial social agent, and ascertain that touch (vs no touch) is the only difference between experimental conditions.

The present study will focus on the effects of interpersonal touch in VR as persuasive technology. Specifically, we will study whether the effects of social touch on shopping behavior (as found by Hornik, 1991, [9]) can also be found in VR. Therefore, the current research will study what the effects are of artificial social touch versus no touch on (shopping) behavior in virtual reality. Based on the theories and research findings presented above, we expected that participants who are touched by the artificial agent in VR will spend more time (H1), and more money (H2), in the virtual shop, and that they also will evaluate the shopping experience more positively (H3).

2   Method

2.1   Participants and Experiment Design

A total of forty-four participants (30 male and 14 female; 28 Chinese, 10 Dutch, 2 Irish, 2 American, 1 Indonesian and 1 Slovak, aged 18 to 34 years old) were recruited via Facebook, among TU/e students and among visitors at Enversed VR Center. Power analysis indicated that a minimal sample size of 44 was necessary to provide 90% power when expecting a medium effect size ($f = 0.25$), using alpha error level of $p < 0.05$. All participants participated in both two experimental conditions (touch and no touch), in random order. For their participation of approximately 12 min, participants were rewarded with a small gift.

2.2   Procedure

After agreeing to participate and reading and signing an informed consent form, participants were explained that in this experiment, they were going to visit three virtual shops. The first one was a training shop (a virtual grocery store) where they learned the basic operations of picking up items, checking out and answering questions in VR. The other two were a stationery shop (see Fig. 3) and a book shop (see Fig. 1). After the training shop, participants experienced both the experimental condition and control condition in a random order. In the experimental condition, participants were touched (on the left upper arm) in the shop by the virtual shop assistant. In the control condition, participants were not touched. The experimental condition was presented randomly in either the stationery shop or the book shop.

Participants were instructed to buy one item in each shop and try to control the money they spent (in each shop) to around €4.50.

When entering the shop in both the experimental and the control condition, participants started at position A (see Fig. 2), and the virtual shop assistant was at position B, facing the participant, and the (female) shopping assistant greeted the participant. In the experimental condition, the shop assistant greeted the participants, saying "Welcome to our store", and extended her arm touching the participant on the left upper arm (using the actuator described in the Materials section). In the control condition, the shop assistant identically greeted the participant but refrained from any touching behavior.

Next, the shop assistant walked to the corner of the shop (position C in Fig. 2) and stayed there (looking around casually) for the remainder of the shopping experience. Participants could start shopping after being greeted. There was a self-checkout machine by the entrance. When participants finished shopping in the virtual shop, they had to check out by touching the screen of the checkout machine (see Fig. 3). After each shop, participants were kindly asked to answer a few questions in VR, to evaluate the shop, the shop assistant and the shopping experience. After the seven questions, participants were directed automatically to the starting point of the next shop.

2.3   Materials

The three virtual shops were created in Unreal Engine 4 [6]. Each of them had a (virtual and real) dimension of 5 m by 4 m (see Figs. 1 and 3), and shared the same floor plan (see Fig. 2).

Fig. 1. Book shop

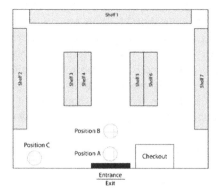

Fig. 2. Floor plan

There were 10 kinds of items in each shop, and the price range in the three shops was identical (from €1.59 to €7.99) with the same average price ($M = 4.4$, $SD = 2.02$). Two different female shop assistants were used (at random) in the two stores (see Fig. 3).

Fig. 3. Stationery shop with the virtual shop assistant

To provide the feeling of being touched, participants were asked to wear a specially developed arm band during the whole experiment. This arm band consisted of a stretching cloth band, equipped with a small motor controlled by a microprocessor (see Fig. 4). The touching arm was 41 mm long, 3.5 mm thick and was attached to the motor which rotated 60° providing 0.08 N force on the arm, its movement synchronized with the animation of the virtual shop assistant. When the virtual assistant raised her arm and reached participants' upper arm, the system triggered the motor on the armband.

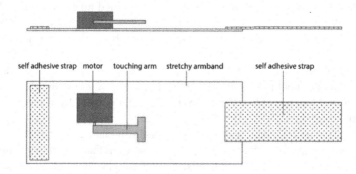

Fig. 4. Special armband to provide the feeling of touch

Background music was used in the experiment in VR. To limit the influence of the music on shopping behavior (see [1, 23]), the present study used piano pieces in low volume, identical in all three stores. It was played on an over-ear headphones that plugged into the VR headset. The volume of the music did not overwhelm the virtual shop assistant's voice, but was loud enough to cover the sound of motor on the touching armband.

2.4 Measures

Shopping time was recorded by the VR system, and started when the participants entered a virtual shop and ended when they checked out. The money they spent in each store was also recorded.

To measure the evaluation by the participant of each shopping experience, a set of seven questions was presented to the participant after every shop. Based other measures assessing experience evaluation (see e.g., [2, 16]), this measure contained questions assessing the participants evaluation of the shopping experience (on pleasure, arousal, satisfaction, valence) and also the shopping assistant. By averaging these seven question, we constructed a reliable measure (*cronbach's alpha* = 0.835) of overall shopping experience evaluation.

3   Results

Multivariate analysis of variance (MANOVA) was used to assess the effects of our independent variable (touch vs no touch) on the three dependent variables (shopping time, money spend, and shopping experience evaluation) using a 2 (touch versus no touch) x 3 (time, price and evaluation) within subjects MANOVA. As expected, the main effect of touch was found for the three dependent variables: results provided evidence that the time participants spent in the virtual shop was longer, the money participants spent in the virtual shop was more, and participants' overall evaluation of the shopping experience was higher, when a participant was touched as compared to when the participant was not touched by the artificial social agent, indicated by a main effect of touch, $F(1, 43) = 4.60$, $p = .038$. Results provided no evidence that this main effect was different for the three types of dependent measures (time, money, and evaluation), as results showed no interaction of touch by type of dependent variable, $F < 1$.

More specifically, first, when a participant was touched by the artificial agent in a VR shop, he or she spent more time ($M = 83.12$ s, $SD = 32.84$) in the shop than when he or she was not touched ($M = 75.64$ s, $SD = 28.21$), indicated by the simple effect of touch for shopping time $F(1, 43) = 3.39$, $p = .072$.

Second, when a participant was touched by the artificial agent in a VR shop, he or she spent more money ($M = 5.81$, $SD = 2.49$) in that shop than when he or she was not touched ($M = 5.02$, $SD = 1.90$), indicated by the simple effect of touch for money spent $F(1, 43) = 4.37$, $p = .043$.

Third, when a participant was touched by the artificial agent in a VR shop, he or she evaluated the shopping experience in that shop more positively ($M = 4.81$, $SD = .96$) than when he or she was not touched ($M = 4.31$, $SD = 1.03$), indicated by the simple effect of touch for overall evaluation $F(1, 43) = 15.46$, $p < .001$.

Furthermore, an analysis including also shop type (stationary shop versus book shop) results showed that participants' responses to touch were different in the two shops. For this, we performed a 2 (shop type) x 2 (touch versus no touch) x 3 (time, price and evaluation) MANOVA. Results suggested that touch influenced time spend in the shop only in the stationary shop, showing that when a participant was touched by the artificial agent in the stationery shop, he or she spent more time ($M = 85.71$ s, $SD = 35.04$) in the shop than when he or she was not touched ($M = 71.87$ s, $SD = 30.83$), indicated by the interaction effect of touch and shop type for shopping time $F(1, 42) = 5.42, p = .025$, while no significant interaction effect for shopping time was found in the book shop $F < 1$.

Also, results suggested that touch influenced amount of spending only in the book shop, showing that when a participant was touched by the artificial agent in the book shop, he or she spent more money ($M = 6.05, SD = 2.76$) in the shop than when he or she was not touched ($M = 4.52, SD = 1.31$), indicated by the interaction effect of touch and shop type for shopping time $F(1, 42) = 9.76$, $p = .003$, while no significant interaction effect for shopping time was found in the stationery shop, $F < 1$.

Third, results provided no evidence that the effect of touch on shopping experience evaluation was different in one of the two shops, as no significant interaction effect of touch and shop type for overall evaluation was found, $F < 1$.

Finally, results provided no evidence that the order in which participants visited the store in which they were touched and the store in which they were not touched influenced the average price of the object they bought, the time they spent in the shop or their evaluation of the shop. To analyze the effect of order, we performed a 2 (shop order) x 2 (touch versus no touch) x 3 (time, price and evaluation) MANOVA, which showed no (interaction) effects of shop order, all p's $> .3$.

4 Conclusion and Discussion

VR technology is developing fast in the recent years and has the potential of having a huge impact on many domains like for example VR shopping. As argued in the Introduction, to our knowledge, earlier research about VR as a persuasive technology is relatively rare, and the persuasive effects in changing behavior of interpersonal touch in VR have not been investigated. Earlier research by Hornik (1991) found that in a real bookstore, a slight touch by a shopping assistant on the shopper's upper arm increased his or her shopping time, amount of shopping, as well as overall evaluation of the shopping experience [9]. Whether (artificial) social touch can have similar effects in VR remained unknown. Therefore, the present study investigated the effects of artificial social touch versus no touch on shopping behavior in VR.

To investigate this question, we set up an experiment in which participants were asked to shop in two virtual shops. In one shop the virtual shop assistant touched participants (shoppers) on the upper arm while greeting. In the other shop the virtual shop assistant identically greeted participants, refraining from any touch. Participants experienced the touch and no touch conditions in a random order.

The results showed that when participants were touched by the virtual shop assistant in a virtual shop, they spent more time in that shop, spent more money on purchasing and the overall evaluation of the shopping experience was more positive. The results were in line with our hypotheses as well as early research by Hornik (1991) conducted in a real bookstore [9]. Our study confirmed Hornik's [9] results, but now in a virtual bookstore and thereby also suggested that although there are differences between the real world environment and our VR environment, the effect of social touch still can occur. Another difference with reality was that in our VR store, participants were instructed to buy one item only, and to spend only a limited amount of money (€4.50). Future research might investigate the effects of artificial social touch on shopping behavior when the shopping situation is more life-like (e.g., when people buy products with their own, limited budgets and time).

The present study was conducted in VR and participants were touched by a virtual shop assistant. The results indicated that participants responded to the touch of the virtual shop assistant as to the touch of a real person. Some participants replied to the virtual shop assistant's greeting by saying "Thank you". Some participants glanced towards the virtual shop assistant during shopping and checkout. Thereby, results confirmed the media equation hypothesis [20]. Participants of different gender and from different countries responded socially to the virtual agent. These response seemed to be natural and automatic, which is in line with the proposal of the media equation hypothesis [20] that social behavior towards technology is mainly automatic, uncontrolled behavior.

So, similar as in the real world, the effect of interpersonal touch was found in the virtual environment. The tactile feedback increased social cue to the artificial social agent and could help to increase participants' perceived realism.

Since artificial social touch has influence on consumers' purchasing behavior in VR and VR shopping is an emerging market, one implication of the current research is that virtual shop assistants that use artificial social touch can be applied in virtual shopping environment. They have the potential to increase sales, shopping time and consumers' evaluation of the virtual shop. Artificial social touch can increase the persuasive power of the virtual shop assistant.

Current results also showed that participants' responses to touch were different in the two shops (the stationary shop and the book shop). We argue that the explanation for this finding is the different characteristics of the items in the two types of stores. That is, in the book shop, all items (books) had similar shapes and sizes, and only the covers of the books were different, while all print on book covers was quite meaningless (e.g., unclear titles). Therefore, spending more time in that store was not very useful, which can explain the lack of an influence of artificial social touch on time spent in the book store, while the prices of books differed allowing participants to respond in a social way to the artificial social touch (by spending a little more money). In the stationary shop, items were much more different from each other and thereby that shop may have been less boring than the book shop. This larger variance between the stationary shop items might have allowed the participants to spend more time (as found) after having been touched by the shopping assistant. The larger diversity of these items may also have increased the influence of a shopper's personal preference on his or her choice of items, thereby limiting the (relative) influence of artificial social touch on their spending.

Future research can investigate various issues in more detail. First, the present study had an unbalanced gender ratio. It is unknown that whether the effect of artificial social touch differs between male and female. Previous research indicated that female respond more positively than male to being touched [24]. Future research can investigate the effect of touch on different genders.

Second, although the effect of touch was found, the underlying psychological mechanism still remained unclear. A possible explanation in line with the media equation hypothesis [20] is that the virtual shop assistant was treated as a social entity, and the virtual shop assistant influences consumers as real sales person. A different type of explanation is that the feeling of touch increased the arousal level of participants so that they stayed longer in the virtual shop and purchased more. Future research can focus on the underlying mechanism by including more conditions, like for example also a condition in which the same feeling is activated (by the actuator) but in such a way that it cannot be ascribed to social touch. Also, such future research could dis-entangle the various elements (and their effects) of greeting behavior by an artificial social agent. For example, future research might study whether the element of bowing towards the customer, or simply spending a little more attention to the customer might already increase purchases.

Third, the meaning of touch can differ from culture to culture. The participants of the present study were mainly Dutch and Chinese, and it remains unclear whether similar effect can be found in other regions and cultures. Future research can investigate the effect of interpersonal touch among different cultures.

In sum, the present research shows that artificial social touch influences consumers' purchasing behavior by increasing their shopping time, the money they spent and the overall evaluation of their shopping experience. Adding to research on the effects of social touch in real life shopping environments (e.g., [9]), the current results present clear evidence that touch behavior and the related tactile stimuli drive these effects on shopping behavior, while excluding other influences (e.g., the shopping assistant smiling while touching). Now VR technology is used in many domains and VR shopping is an emerging market, artificial social agents can be used in VR shopping to influence consumers' purchasing behavior.

Imagine in the near future, if you are shopping in a VR shop that uses symbiotic interactions (see [31]). The virtual shop assistant greets you, and touches you on the upper arm while doing so. You can see the virtual assistant, hear her voice and also feel the touch in VR. Current results show that this artificial social touch may make you stay longer in the VR shop, spent more money and evaluate the shopping experience more positively.

References

1. Areni, C.S., Kim, D.: The influence of background music on shopping behavior: classical versus top-forty music in a wine store. ACR North American Advances (1993)
2. Bradley, M.M.: Emotional memory: a dimensional analysis. In: Emotions: Essays on emotion theory, pp. 97–134 (1994)

3. Burdea, G.C.: Keynote address: haptics feedback for virtual reality. In: Proceedings of International Workshop on Virtual Prototyping. Laval, France (1999)
4. Chittaro, L., Zangrando, N.: The persuasive power of virtual reality: effects of simulated human distress on attitudes towards fire safety. In: Ploug, T., Hasle, P., Oinas-Kukkonen, H. (eds.) PERSUASIVE 2010. LNCS, vol. 6137, pp. 58–69. Springer, Heidelberg (2010). https://doi.org/10.1007/978-3-642-13226-1_8
5. Furnham, A., Petrova, E.: Body Language in Business: Decoding the Signals. Palgrave Macmillan, New York (2010)
6. Game Engine Technology by Unreal. https://www.unrealengine.com/. Accessed 25 Sept 2017
7. Hoffman, H.G.: Physically touching virtual objects using tactile augmentation enhances the realism of virtual environments. In: Virtual Reality Annual International Symposium, 1998. Proceedings., IEEE 1998, pp. 59–63. IEEE (1998)
8. Holzwarth, M., Janiszewski, C., Neumann, M.M.: The influence of avatars on online consumer shopping behavior. J. Market. **70**, 19–36 (2006)
9. Hornik, J.: Shopping time and purchasing behavior as a result of in-store tactile stimulation. Percept. Mot. Skills **73**, 969–970 (1991)
10. Jayaram, S., Connacher, H.I., Lyons, K.W.: Virtual assembly using virtual reality techniques. Comput. Aided Des. **29**, 575–584 (1997)
11. Krijn, M., Emmelkamp, P.M., Olafsson, R.P., Biemond, R.: Virtual reality exposure therapy of anxiety disorders: a review. Clin. Psychol. Rev. **24**, 259–281 (2004)
12. Louwerse, M.M., Graesser, A.C., Lu, S., Mitchell, H.H.: Social cues in animated conversational agents. Appl. Cogn. Psychol. **19**, 693–704 (2005)
13. Mayer, R.E., Sobko, K., Mautone, P.D.: Social cues in multimedia learning: role of speaker's voice. J. Educ. Psychol. **95**, 419 (2003)
14. Mehrabian, A.: Silent Messages, vol. 8. Wadsworth, Belmont (1971)
15. Mehrabian, A., Russell, J.A.: An Approach to Environmental Psychology. The MIT Press, Cambridge (1974)
16. Miller, G.A., Levin, D.N., Kozak, M.J., Cook III, E.W., McLean Jr., A., Lang, P.J.: Individual differences in imagery and the psychophysiology of emotion. Cogn. Emot. **1**, 367–390 (1987)
17. Moon, Y.: Intimate exchanges: using computers to elicit self-disclosure from consumers. J. Consum. Res. **26**, 323–339 (2000)
18. Oculus Rift Homepage, https://www.oculus.com/rift/. Accessed 25 Sept 2017
19. Playstation VR: Homepage, https://www.playstation.com/en-au/explore/playstation-vr/. Accessed 25 Sept 2017
20. Reeves, B., Nass, C.: How people treat computers, television, and new media like real people and places, pp. 3–18. CSLI Publications and Cambridge university press (1996)
21. Robert, D., John, R.: Store atmosphere: an environmental psychology approach. J. Retail. **58**, 34–57 (1982)
22. Roubroeks, M., Ham, J., Midden, C.: When artificial social agents try to persuade people: the role of social agency on the occurrence of psychological reactance. Int. J. Social Robot. **3**, 155–165 (2011)
23. Smith, P.C., Curnow, R.: "Arousal hypothesis" and the effects of music on purchasing behavior. J. Appl. Psychol. **50**, 255 (1966)
24. Stier, D.S., Hall, J.A.: Gender differences in touch: an empirical and theoretical review. J. Pers. Soc. Psychol. **47**, 440 (1984)
25. Våpenstad, C., Hofstad, E.F., Langø, T., Mårvik, R., Chmarra, M.K.: Perceiving haptic feedback in virtual reality simulators. Surg. Endosc. **27**, 2391–2397 (2013)

26. Vive | Discover Virtual Reality Beyond Imagination Homepage, https://www.vive.com/eu/. Accessed 25 Sept 2017
27. Webster Jr, F.E.: Interpersonal communication and salesman effectiveness. J. Market. 7–13 (1968)
28. Wycoff, E.B., Holley, J.D.: Effects of flight attendants' touch upon airline passengers' perceptions of the attendant and the airline. Percept. Mot. Skills **71**, 932–934 (1990)
29. Gallace, A., Spence, C.: The science of interpersonal touch: an overview. Neurosci. Biobehav. Rev. **34**(2), 246–259 (2008)
30. Haans, A., IJsselsteijn, W.: Mediated social touch: a review of current research and future directions. Virtual Reality **9**(2–3), 149–159 (2006)
31. Jacucci, G., Spagnolli, A., Freeman, J., Gamberini, L.: Symbiotic interaction: a critical definition and comparison to other human-computer paradigms. In: Jacucci, G., Gamberini, L., Freeman, J., Spagnolli, A. (eds.) Symbiotic 2014. LNCS, vol. 8820, pp. 3–20. Springer, Cham (2014). https://doi.org/10.1007/978-3-319-13500-7_1

Author Index

Printed in the United States
By Bookmasters